KABUKI
BACKSTAGE, ONSTAGE

KABUKI
BACKSTAGE, ONSTAGE
An Actor's Life

Matazo Nakamura

Translated by Mark Oshima

KODANSHA INTERNATIONAL
Tokyo and New York

Endpapers: A series of prints by Utagawa Kunisada depicting the back-stage third floor of the Ichimura-za, Edo (in what is today Ningyo-cho), 1813. At that time the stars' dressing rooms were located on the third floor.
Front left: The actor standing (*center*) is Bando Mitsugoro III, Mitsugoro VIII's distant family relation and direct artistic ancestor. Note the *deshi* (assistants) at smaller mirrors along the side of the room, and (*lower*) *onnagata* emerging from their second-floor dressing room.
Front right: Note the portrait of Tsuruya Namboku on the right, the *onnagata* on the stairs and in the foreground, and the actors with the Ichikawa family crest of three concentric squares on their clothes.
Back right: The upper half of the print shows Ichikawa Danjuro VII's dressing room. The actor is sitting in front of a mirror inscribed with the Danjuro family crest. He is wearing *kumadori* makeup and is surrounded by patrons. The lower part of the print shows the dressing room of Iwai Hanshiro V, a famous *onnagata* (*center*), shared by other *onnagata* of the same line.

Kabuki Backstage, Onstage was originally published as *Shirazā itte kikaseyashō* by Nihon Television in 1988.

Distributed in the United States by Kodansha International/ USA Ltd., 114 Fifth Avenue, New York, New York 10011. Published by Kodansha International Ltd 17-14, Otowa 1-chome, Bunkyo-ku, Tokyo 112 and Kodansha International/ USA Ltd., 114 Fifth Avenue, New York, New York 10011. Copyright © 1988 Matazo Nakamura. English translation © 1990 Mark Oshima. All rights reserved. Printed in Japan.

Library of Congress Cataloging-in-Publication Data
Nakamura, Matazo, 1933-
   (Shirazā itte kikaseyashō. English)
   Kabuki backstage, onstage/by Matazo
   Nakamura: translated by Mark Oshima.—1st ed.
   p. cm.
   Translation of: Shirazā itte kikaseyashō
   Includes bibliographical references.
   1. Nakamura, Matazo, 1933- 2. Actors—Japan—
   Biography. 3. Kabuki I. Title.
   PN2928.N283A3 1990
   792'.028'092—dc20   90-4099

ISBN 0-87011-985-0 (U.S.)
ISBN 4-7700-1485-6 (Japan)

First edition, 1990

Contents

Glossary

Aragoto   Heroic acting style developed in the late 17th century by Ichikawa Danjuro I.

Gakuya   Dressing room. This term is used for the entire backstage area.

Geza   The musicians' room; it is located behind a black grille on the stage, to the left of the audience.

Gidayu   Also called *takemoto*; the narrative music from the bunraku puppet theater. In kabuki it is used especially in plays from the puppet repertory.

Hakama   A divided skirt, or long culottes.

Hanamichi   The runway through the audience; used as an extension of the acting space.

Iemoto   The head of an artistic family or school. In kabuki the *iemoto* system means that the heads of leading families have almost total control over the art form.

Juhachiban   A collection of plays that are the specialty of the Ichikawa Danjuro family. Literally "eighteen plays," the term implies "best" eighteen. The collection includes *Kanjincho* and *Shibaraku*.

Koken   Assistants who appear on stage to take care of an actor's props and costumes.

Kumadori   Distinctive makeup style with lines—usually red to indicate strength—on a white base. This style originated with *aragoto* acting.

Mie   Dramatic poses that punctuate kabuki movement.

Nadai   Rank of a full-fledged actor; the term is used to distinguish these actors from lower-ranking actors who must use the mass dressing room.

Nagauta   Lyrical singing style used both as the accompaniment for some dance scenes and as background music from the *geza*.

Obeya   The collective dressing room on the third floor of the theater assigned to low-ranking actors.

Onnagata   All actors in kabuki are male. *Onnagata* are actors who specialize in female roles.

Seiza   Formal kneeling; this sitting style is an important part of both polite Japanese behavior and kabuki movement.

Suri ashi   Basic sliding step in traditional Japanese theater.

Tachimawari   Stylized fight scenes.

Taiko   Stick drum; also part of the noh percussion ensemble.

Tokiwazu   Style of narrative music that originated in 18th-century Edo. It accompanies dance scenes and is never used with puppets.

Tsuzumi   Hand drums that are also part of the noh percussion ensemble. There are two types, the *kotsuzumi* or "small drum" which is held on the shoulder and the *otsuzumi* or "large drum" which is held on the lap.

Yago   A name used for groups of actors which ends in "ya," an ending also used for the names of shops.

Preface

Reflecting the variety of the circumstances that inspired it, this book is essentially a collection of self-contained essays, linked by my wish to explain as clearly as possible what exactly kabuki is, and how economic and dramatic developments have contributed to its present nature.

The book began as a series of chats on a television program, but it soon grew into a text, a record of what I teach at Showa Music Conservatory and elsewhere about kabuki. But I am not primarily an educator. First and foremost I am a kabuki actor.

This year I am appearing in performances of kabuki at the National Theater and also, as an actor under contract to the Toho production company, I appear in modern plays that use actresses instead of *onnagata*. In addition, this year I went to West Germany and to Queen Margaret College in Scotland to teach kabuki. Part of this book, for example the short syllabus at the end, comes from my experiences teaching abroad. When I went to the University of Munich in early 1982, I was asked if I had a textbook of kabuki. I didn't, so on my return to Japan I began writing. When I went to West Berlin the following year at the invitation of Dr. Manfred Linke of the International Theater Institute, I brought a small booklet with texts in English and German to use as a textbook.

Kabuki Backstage, Onstage was also written to accompany my kabuki workshops. Each year I do more and more kabuki demonstrations, or workshops, for foreigners living in Tokyo. I hold the workshops at places like the Foreign Correspondents'

Club of Japan, or International House, and employ Mark Oshima, the translator of this book, as an interpreter. During these demonstrations, as described in the text, I put on my costume and makeup in front of the audience, and always end with a question and answer period.

Finally I would like to thank Mark Oshima for his translation and help in adapting the book, especially the Introduction and *Gakuya* chapters, to meet foreigners' needs, and Tazawa Yuzo and Prue Moodie, my editors at Kodansha International, for making this book possible.

Nakamura Matazo
April 1990, Tokyo

Editor's note: Japanese names appear in the traditional order, i.e., family name followed by given name. Following the general practice, kabuki actors are usually referred to by given name only.

Introduction

Ginza, Tokyo's most prestigious shopping district, is crammed with elegant department stores, and small specialty shops selling kimonos, cameras and pearls. At its eastern end is the gray bulk of a large ferro-concrete theater. This more or less modern, Western-style structure is embellished with traditional Japanese tiled gables, and, on festive occasions, right above the main entrance there is a kind of turret, wrapped in a blue cloth with the bold pattern of a crane, topped with ceremonial lances from which white manes hang down over the sidewalk below.

In the Edo period (1603–1868), these spears indicated that a theater had official permission from the shogunate to operate. In Edo (the former name for Tokyo), there were just three theaters accorded this privilege. Today, long after the days of the shogunate, this theater, the Kabuki-za, continues to present the art form that gave it its name, keeping the world of Edo Japan alive on a reduced scale.

To venture inside the theater is to see some of the wide variety of plays in the kabuki repertoire. For example, the stage may be set in the courtyard of an imposing shrine. The villain is a court noble who has usurped power over the land and plans to seal his power with a ceremonial gift of a precious sword to the state shrine. He sits center stage, resplendent in white silk robes, the bulk of his head emphasized by an enormous wig and plow-shaped whiskers. His face is covered with bold blue lines—the *kumadori* makeup that is one of the most instantly recognizable features of kabuki. The lines indicate great strength, and the

11

blue color indicates that he is an evil court noble. Arrayed in front of him are the treasures that he is about to present to the shrine and behind him, in forced perspective, we see the distant shrine building. He is surrounded by his supporters, including a priest with a shaven head and two long, odd catfish-like whiskers, and a female warrior. Lined up behind him are warriors that look rather like sumo wrestlers with red faces and enormous, grotesque bellies.

This is the setting for the play *Shibaraku* (Wait a Moment!). The opening lines of the play are rather tedious, but the color and spectacle of its staging are mind-boggling. The action builds up to one climactic moment. The villain orders the prince and princess—virtuous characters who have attempted to impede his rise to power—executed, and, as swords are raised to behead them, a voice thunders from the back of the theater, *Shibaraku!* The swords stop, and those wielding them wonder who could be calling to them to stop. Nothing further happens so they raise their swords again, and once more the call of *Shibaraku!* resounds through the theater.

Finally we see the owner of the voice, the hero of the play, Kamakura Gongoro. He is an imposing sight as he makes his entrance along the *hanamichi* runway, which passes through the audience. His body is heavily padded to create the impression of massive power and strength. He wears a short robe over an armored breastplate and armguards. The sleeves of this robe are tied back with enormous cords made of thick purple and blue strands of silk twisted together. On top of this he wears a full-sleeve padded kimono, and finally, a persimmon-colored long *hakama* (a kind of long, full culottes) and an overrobe with huge square sleeves stiffened with bamboo frames, making them look like enormous square shields. The crest displayed on these sleeves—three concentric rice measures outlined in white—is that of the the Danjuro line of the Ichikawa family, the principal acting line in kabuki. The actor's face is made up, using the *kumadori* technique, in a pattern of bold red lines over a white base indicating the character's virtue and strength. His wildly exaggerated sidelocks are made of hair hardened with wax and polished to form shiny black columns that stick out from his face.

Kamakura Gongoro has come to save the day and punctuates

his actions with powerful poses, screwing his face into an imposing expression made even more fierce by crossing his eyes at the
climactic moment. After defeating the villain's allies, Gongoro
takes on a large crowd of his minions, beheads them all with one
sweep of his long sword, and exits in triumph.

   Shibaraku is not really a play, it is a kind of routine that was
inserted into all kinds of plays as a showcase for members of the
Danjuro line of actors. The wild exaggeration of costume and
makeup, and the earth-shattering voice of Kamakura Gongoro
make this role representative of the bombastic *aragoto* style of acting, a style of acting created by Ichikawa Danjuro at the beginning of the eighteenth century. It conveys the spirit of early
Edo, which had just become the political center of Japan, and
was still something of a frontier town full of samurai.

   Not only was the role of Kamakura Gongoro traditionally
reserved for Danjuro, but all the roles in this play, and indeed in
any kabuki play, are taken only by actors of a certain status. The
role of the villain is very prestigious, and the roles of the catfish
priest, female warrior and the innocent victims are always
played by top stars. The warriors are played by minor actors
who have reached the rank of *nadai,* and the minions are played
by actors who are at the bottom of the ladder despite the
strength and agility that they need for the acrobatics of the fight
scenes.

   This is an example of kabuki's highly stylized period pieces,
but we might also catch a glimpse of a domestic drama, perhaps
a love suicide play. Instead of the colorful spectacle of *Shibaraku*
we see the humble everyday life of commoners, and the problem of a couple that cannot be united, perhaps a married merchant and the courtesan that he loves. If they cannot be
together in life, they will seek unity in death and hope to be
reborn together. The greatest love suicide plays were written by
Chikamatsu Monzaemon (1653–1724) for the bunraku puppet
theater, and even though the kabuki versions use live actors,
they retain the bunraku tradition of narrator and shamisen
player accompanying the action.

   The lyrical highpoint of a love suicide play is the final
michiyuki or travelling scene. The couple dress in their finest
clothes, and the drab realism of the preceding scenes changes to

heightened poetic drama, giving a kind of heroic, noble stature to these unfortunate commoners. The *michiyuki* scenes are rich and dream-like, showing the characters at some indefinable point between life and death. In *Sonezaki Shinju* (The Love Suicide at Sonezaki), Chikamatsu's first love suicide play, the narrator chants the beautiful lines: "Farewell to this world. Farewell to this night. What are we that travel on our way to death? We are no more than frost on the road to the graveyard, vanishing with each step. How sad this life, this dream within a dream." The two lovers walk quietly, hand in hand, gazing at one another intently since this will be their last moment together. The actors move with expressive dance gestures as the narrator chants their story.

"Actors" is the correct word since there are no actresses in kabuki. All female roles are played by actors called *onnagata* who specialize in such roles. The highly sophisticated repertory of feminine movements for the *onnagata* is an important part of the technical resources of kabuki—and one of the most difficult and painful skills to acquire, since *onnagata* movement emphasizes graceful poses that are excruciating to perform.

If *aragoto* epitomizes early Edo, the puppet plays of Chikamatsu epitomize the culture of early Osaka, a city of merchants that was prosperous long before the rise of Edo. In fact, although Edo was the political center, the cultural center was in western Japan, the cities of Kyoto and Osaka in the region that was known as *kamigata* or "the upper region" because Kyoto was the exalted home of the emperor. Kamigata continued to be the cultural center of Japan until well into the eighteenth century.

Not all domestic plays are serious and tragic like Chikamatsu's love suicide plays. We might catch a glimpse of *Benten Kozo* (Benten, the Thief), a late nineteenth-century play. A well-dressed young girl sits in the middle of a dry goods store with a male attendant. Suddenly the head clerk sees her slip some cloth into her kimono. He and the other clerks accuse her of shoplifting and beat her, leaving an ugly gash on her forehead where she was hit with an abacus. The girl's attendant proves that the cloth she was accused of taking had been bought at another store, and the unfortunate store-owner must now come up with some appropriate payment to compensate her and to keep the incident quiet. The girl and her companion are about to leave with the money when a samurai comes out from the back of the store and asks them to stay for a moment. He says that he noticed that the girl had a tattoo and suspects that she is a man in disguise. This is the highlight of the scene. One moment the girl is huddling on the floor, pressing a cloth to her wound, the very picture of distressed femininity. Then, as Benten Kozo realizes that he has been exposed, the actor's movements change subtly and he begins to move like a man, a rough thief. The shop people have no idea who he is, so Benten Kozo announces grandly, "If you don't know, let me tell you just who I am," and delivers the role's most famous speech, a rhythmical poetic piece in which he describes his birth, upbringing, and how he became a thief. Finally Benten Kozo and his companion talk their way out of the situation and leave, promising to return. The role of Benten Kozo combines *onnagata* acting with male acting and requires a star actor capable of projecting immense rascally charm.

Another possibility would be to find the stage set with scenery representing plain boards all around, with a single gnarled pine painted on the center of the back wall and a few bamboos on either side. This setting is used for plays adapted directly from the classic noh theater. While kabuki flourished in the seventeenth to nineteenth centuries, a period full of change and energy, noh was developed in the fourteenth century at the court of the Muromachi shogun Yoshimitsu. After that, noh became the art form of the samurai class, and this stately theater with its masks and refined singing and movement became largely frozen. Although it was heavily patronized by the samurai class during the Edo period, few new plays were written and it became a fixed, classical art, while kabuki continually changed and developed.

Commoners rarely had a chance to see a performance of noh, since it remained very much the preserve of the samurai class. Nonetheless, beginning in the nineteenth century, much of the material for the early kabuki plays was derived from the noh repertoire. Even the simple noh stage setting was reproduced, although it acquired something of the flamboyance of kabuki in the process. Probably the most famous and popular of the plays

adapted from noh is *Kanjincho* (The Subscription List), a kabuki
version of the noh play *Ataka*.

The play is one of many about the twelfth-century general,
Minamoto no Yoshitsune. He was instrumental in making his
half brother, Yoritomo, the first shogun, but Yoritomo soon
grew suspicious of him. *Kanjincho* relates the story of Yoshitsune's flight from the capital, aided by Benkei, a warrior-priest
of great strength and ingenuity. Yoshitsune and his followers are
disguised as *yamabushi* or mountain priests, but Yoritomo has
heard about this and has had barriers set up on all the major
roads to stop all travelers, especially *yamabushi*. The play is
about Benkei's confrontation with a high-ranking samurai
named Togashi who is in charge of the barrier at a place called
Ataka. Togashi suspects that these are the men he is seeking,
but Benkei foils his every question. One of the high points of
the play is when Togashi says that if they are who they say they
are, priests collecting funds for rebuilding the great temple of
Todaiji, they must have a subscription list, a document from the
imperial court giving them permission to collect funds. Benkei
takes a blank scroll and begins to read. Togashi creeps forward,
sees that the scroll is blank and he and Benkei pose tensely, each
looking at the other. Benkei continues to read, making up the or-
nate and obscure language of a typical subscription list as he
goes. Togashi may have been ordered to stop Yoshitsune, but he
is fascinated to see how far Benkei is willing and able to go to
protect his master. Finally, in the face of such devotion Togashi
admits defeat and allows them to pass, first treating Benkei to a
drinking party and asking him to dance. As Yoshitsune's party
leaves, Togashi faces certain death for failing in his duty, and
Benkei, relieved to have gotten through such a dangerous situation watches Yoshitsune and his followers go down the road and
then hurries to catch up with them, rushing down the *hanamichi* runway with a spectacular jumping step called a *roppo*.

Kanjincho is an example of a noh play adapted slightly, and
livened up with kabuki dance and diction. But most kabuki use
of noh is much more fluid, using a story line here, a snatch of
famous text there, or perhaps introducing a short noh-style performance as a play within a play. Perhaps the most familiar example of the free style of adaptation is the dance play *Musume*

Dojoji, the greatest of all kabuki dances, and the pinnacle of the art of the *onnagata.*

In the original Dojoji story, a young girl (some versions say a widow) falls in love with a priest on pilgrimage. He says that he cannot meet with her until he returns from his pilgrimage, but on his return journey he hurries by and does not stop. When the woman hears this, she is filled with jealous fury and pursues him. Finally, at the Hidaka river, her jealousy turns her into a serpent and she goes to Dojoji temple, where the object of her affections is hiding, and coils herself around the bell where he is concealed. Both the man and the bell are destroyed by flames.

The noh play presents Dojoji temple on the occasion of the dedication of a new bell. The abbot of the temple has left strict orders that no women are to be allowed into the temple precincts, but a woman, a court dancer or *shirabyoshi,* comes and talks her way into the temple to dance for the dedication. As she dances, all the priests fall asleep and the woman, who is the ghost of the serpent that destroyed the bell in the first place, takes advantage of their sleep to destroy the hateful bell once more.

In the kabuki version, the overall format is retained, but the scene bears only the vaguest resemblance to the original. The scene becomes the occasion for a spectacular series of dances, using a variety of props, including a silk cloth, a pair of flat red hats that unfold to reveal a whole line of overlapping hats, reminiscent of the scales a snake, and a pair of tambourines whose rattling sound also suggests serpents.

This kind of free adaptation of noh is the norm in kabuki, where, without losing the significance of the original noh plot, a play like Dojoji becomes the occasion for kabuki dance.

A brief look at these various plays, *Shibaraku, Sonezaki Shinju, Benten Kozo, Kanjincho* and *Musume Dojoji* reveals the truly amazing range of skills that the kabuki actor is expected to have. Dance, music, dramatic delivery of lines: all of these are basic skills for the kabuki actor. How do actors acquire these skills and carry on the tradition of centuries? And, for that matter, how has kabuki continued to be produced in the modern world?

In Edo there were three theaters licensed to perform kabuki. Today—but for different reasons—there are also three production organizations involved with kabuki, two giant entertainment companies, Shochiku and Toho, and the Japanese government, in the form of the National Theater.

Unlike many traditional theaters, the Kabuki-za is largely run by a commercial entertainment company, called Shochiku. For ten months of the year the stage of the Kabuki-za is filled with programs of kabuki, which change each month. Nearly all kabuki actors are with Shochiku, which has virtually monopolized kabuki in the twentieth century, despite several challenges. One of the most notable challenges to Shochiku came from its bitter rival Toho. Both companies are vast complexes of entertainment enterprises, including theaters, theater production and film, but while kabuki is the pride and joy of Shochiku, the jewel in Toho's crown is the Takarazuka theater, a kind of musical review in which both male and female roles are played by women. The most important theaters run by Shochiku are at the eastern end of Ginza; the most important theaters run by Toho, including Takarazuka, are at the western end of Ginza.

The National Theater is a twenty-minute walk away on the other side of the Imperial Palace. It is a huge, brown, concrete version of the old log-cabin style of construction used for imperial storehouses. Inside it are some of the finest stage resources in Tokyo, good rehearsal spaces, and rooms for a training program for young actors. But, perhaps because it is so heavily influenced by government bureaucracy, it does not feel very much like a theater. Its programs are also very different from those at the Kabuki-za, since it tries to revive and preserve seldom performed plays.

The Kabuki-za presents selections of plays that are likely to draw a commercial audience. Today, Toho almost never presents kabuki, but the National Theater is interested in preserving and continuing kabuki. The interests of the three producing organizations are quite different, but the pool of kabuki actors is the same. With a few significant exceptions, virtually all of the actors are affiliated with the Shochiku organization. When Toho or the National Theater wants to put on a kabuki performance, it must borrow actors from Shochiku.

Among the exceptions are my teacher, Nakamura Matagoro, and myself, and we are still affiliated with Toho, the result of a historic split in the kabuki world. My career in the kabuki world has been rather unusual, but for that very reason perhaps I can see it and its traditions from an independent perspective. In this book I will look at the world of kabuki past and present, show how this traditional art form has survived and flourished in the modern world, and share my experience in teaching kabuki in Japan and abroad.

Nakamura Shikan II, later to become Nakamura Utaemon IV. This print, by Utagawa Kunisada, was made in 1818 to commemorate Shikan's last performance in Edo before returning to Osaka. His *deshi* (assistant) is behind him. Note the wig for a male role beside him, and the crossed scrolls crest of the Utaemon line on the back of the mirror. Courtesy of the National Museum of Ethnology, Leiden.

CHAPTER 1

A Short History of Kabuki

It is said that kabuki began in the early Edo period (1603–1868), when a woman named Izumo Okuni began to dance something called "Okuni kabuki" in the ancient capital of Kyoto. She danced on the dry riverbed of the Kamo river, the main river running through Kyoto, at the spot where Shijo Bridge crosses it. The entertainment area of old Kyoto has long since been built over and now, between the throngs of passersby and the blocks of buildings that occupy the area, there is no clue as to where Okuni's theater might have been. The only trace is a marker commemorating the birthplace of kabuki in front of the kabuki theater Minami-za, right next to the river.

Even if we don't know where Okuni's theater was, kabuki actors are fond of the venerable Minami-za, since it is where actors go every year for the *kaomise*, a program that in the old days served to introduce the actors for the year's productions, and even now is the most lavish kabuki production in Kyoto. There was once another small theater across the street from Minami-za called Kita-za. But now there is a modern building in its place with nothing to suggest how deeply this area is tied to the roots of kabuki.

The three Chinese characters now used to write the word "kabuki" are *ka* (歌) meaning "song," *bu* (舞) meaning "dance," and *ki* (伎) meaning "skill." But these are a later invention. The word "kabuki" comes from the verb *kabuku* which meant "to lean." It also carried the meaning of something off-beat or deviating from the main path. In other words, kabuki did not mean "song, dance, and acting," but "off-beat performance."

21

A modern equivalent of what was originally meant by kabuki style might be fashionable young people strutting through the streets, or rock music fans with long dyed hair dressed in crazy fashions. In the early Edo period they called young people who were extreme in this way kabuki *mono* (kabuki types). They spent their time partying and enjoying themselves.

When these kabuki *mono* paraded down the street, they had a special proud gait, which looked rather decadent to more sober people. But the style was also, of course, considered hip and exciting.

Kabuki dance (*odori*) was the first to incorporate these elements while they were fresh. A similar effect could be gained by taking the styles and fashions of young people in Tokyo today—in the trendy night spots of Roppongi, or people dancing to rock bands in the street at Omote Sando—and putting them into dance performances.

The kabuki *odori* that Okuni started was a hit among young people of the time, and gradually her popularity increased. Pictures of Okuni show her wearing a *hachimaki* (a kind of headband), a bandanna, a necklace with a large crucifix, a long dress and bracelets jangling on her arms. This was an outlandish costume, based on a magpie-like fashion sense. The source for imported fashions was Portugal, and Okuni was the first to take advantage of new themes and artifacts.

As Izumo Okuni's dances won popularity she gradually gained imitators among the *yuna*, or bathhouse girls. In the early Edo period, one of the amusements for the pleasure-seeking kabuki *mono* was to go to public baths and enjoy the company of bathhouse women who would wash and massage their customers. They entertained the men in a variety of ways, including kabuki dance.

Even though we associate the birth of kabuki with Izumo Okuni, there were probably many skilled dancers like her at the time. It is probably best to think that their collective talent gave rise to kabuki. Compared to professional dancers of Okuni's level, the *yuna* were no more than second-rate imitations. There was probably no particular artistic merit to their dance, and because, unlike Okuni, they did not train and strive for artistic excellence, their dances could not hold an audience for long.

Ultimately they had to rely on their feminine charms, and their so-called kabuki dance became something akin to a strip show.

When this licentious state of affairs forced itself to the attention of the authorities, the shogunate banned *onna joruri* (women storytellers), *onna kabuki* (female kabuki), and *onna mai* (female dancers), declaring all forms of popular entertainment involving female performers a danger to public morals. In 1629 an edict was issued forbidding women to act on stage, dance, or appear on the kabuki stage in any form moving with or without music, under threat of arrest and punishment.

In the Edo period Kyoto was the seat of the imperial court and the cultural capital of Japan, whereas the political center was Edo, home of the shogun. In theory the shogun was simply the most important military official serving a sacred emperor, but in fact the position was that of the head of a ruling government which strictly controlled a powerless and impoverished Imperial court. The story of kabuki follows the center of power east from Kyoto, to the seat of the shogunate in Edo.

Even before the public morals edict was issued, theaters in Edo and Kyoto alike were regulated by the shogunate. Actors and other entertainers were of low social status, since they had no place in the Edo-period social hierarchy of samurai, farmer, craftsman, merchant. Sumptuary laws governed all aspects of people's lives, including the style and color of clothes permissible for each class. These restrictions applied to stage costumes as well, with regulations on acceptable patterns and colors (in particular, purple, and a red the shade of plum blossoms, were forbidden). The restrictions remained in force throughout the Edo period (1600–1867)—for example, the early nineteenth-century kabuki actor Ichikawa Danjuro VII was temporarily exiled from Edo for a violation of these laws.

Theaters could not operate without a license. The four original Edo theaters were the Yamamura-za, the Ichimura-za, the Nakamura-za, and the Morita-za, and up until the order of 1629 banning female performers, they offered plays performed by both actors and actresses. To conform to the new regulation and retain their licenses, the theaters could then only present male actors.

It was difficult to present theater with only men performing, but kabuki theater was already highly developed and could not be easily abandoned. With the permission of the shogunate it had four flourishing theaters and loyal and influential patrons. So female roles were given to attractive boys. This "Youth Kabuki," (*wakashu*) came in its turn to be seen as a threat to public morals, for in a samurai world that tolerated and even idealized certain types of homosexual relationships, the new *wakashu* stars became the objects of intense admiration. Fights would even break out over the youths. In 1652, *wakashu* kabuki was also banned.

The kabuki theaters responded to this development by having the adolescent actors shave off their forelocks so that they looked like adults. This new form was called *yaro kabuki* (male kabuki) and was a far cry from the charms of the two previous varieties. But in time the art of the *onnagata*, or female role specialist, developed and flourished. Kabuki became a complex dramatic art with men playing both male and female roles, a tradition maintained today.

In the early years in Edo kabuki had to contend with other attempts by the authorities to discredit and modify it. After a huge fire in 1657 the theaters were moved out of the center of the city and relocated in a specially designated area on the outskirts. Next the kabuki world was rocked by the "Ejima Incident" of 1714, when a high-ranking woman serving in the women's quarters of the Shogun's palace was found to be having an affair with a kabuki actor named Ejima. Ejima was exiled, and the Yamamura-za, the theater where the couple's affair had been conducted, was closed. Anyone who had abetted the two was sought out and punished. The Yamamura-za never reopened, leaving the Nakamura-za, the Ichimura-za, and the Morita-za to carry on as the major theaters under the shoguns' rule.

Despite the fact that bans on forms of kabuki theater were issued twice in the first half century from its beginning, and that it remained under the continuous scrutiny and control of the shogunate, kabuki clung stubbornly to life, and continued to grow and develop as a dramatic form.

Noh and Kabuki

The stately classical noh theater originated in the fourteenth century as an art form for warriors, and in the Edo period it continued to be a theater for the elite ruling samurai class. Kabuki, on the other hand, was for commoners, and is more colorful and flamboyant. They both draw on long folk traditions, but are very different in nature. Noh is characterized by the kind of movement called *mai* while kabuki is characterized by the kind of movement called *odori*. In everyday conversation the verbs *mau* and *odoru* are both used to mean "to dance" and are sometimes confused. But in the world of the traditional performing arts they mean entirely different things.

Noh comes from the earlier folk traditions of *sarugaku* and *dengaku*, and within these traditions there are many motions which seem to derive from the movements of agriculture, such as the growing of rice seedlings. When handling these seedlings one has to walk around in a flooded rice field. In bare feet the farmers would get stuck in the mud, so they wear clogs called *ta geta* or shoes called *ganjiki*. To move while wearing these one has to use the same sliding steps as those called *suri ashi* in noh. The hips are drawn back and one bends slightly at the waist in order to walk sliding one's feet along the ground.

The critic and theater director, Takechi Tetsuji, saw this movement as the origin of *suri ashi* in noh, but it could even be seen as the origin of *mai* itself, since *mai* implies a dance characterized by this sliding step. In *mai*, the dancer never jumps into the air. In other words, a *mai* dancer moves smoothly and heavily, keeping the center of gravity low, his body always in contact with the ground. The dances of noh tend to consist of smooth circling movements with sliding steps.

By contrast, *odoru* means to move with vigor—using stamps and exaggerated gesture. Even if there is none of the spectacular jumps and leaps of ballet, *odori* has the performer constantly lifting his feet off the ground. The dancer stamps out a rhythm, perhaps reminiscent of the feet of an ancient iron worker pumping the pedal of a bellows.

The old work songs are good candidates for the origin of some of the characteristics of kabuki dance. Izumo Okuni developed her dances at a time when iron sand had been discovered along the Japan Sea coast in the area that is now Tottori and Shimane prefectures. The tedious labor of extracting the iron by continually treading the muddy sand was almost impossible to keep up without combining it with song and rhythmical repetition of meaningless syllables like *enya kore dokkoisho*. Many other work songs could be heard regularly until quite recently. When I was a boy we chanted a similar refrain when everyone worked together to stamp down the ground to ensure a firm foundation for a house about to be built.

Noh drama was accompanied by an ensemble of flute, stick drum, small hand drum and large hand drum. The ensemble for early kabuki was similar, adding only a few simple percussion instruments. Instead of the complexity of noh, the kabuki ensemble produced simple, song-like melodies and rhythms. Okuni also used a small gong called a *kane*. Small enough to fit in the hand, it was the kind of gong that was used by street peddlers to attract customers and it may also have been used by Buddhist monks. With this kind of musical accompaniment, Okuni's dances must have been extremely lively.

Today, the basic instrument of the kabuki theater is the three stringed *shamisen*. It has a small, square body made of wood and covered with cat skin, and is played with an ivory plectrum. It produces a pungent sound somewhat reminiscent of a banjo, and punctuates both lyrical and narrative forms of singing. In its original form, in Okinawa, it was called the *jabisen* and was covered with snake skin. It was introduced to kabuki somewhat after the time of Izumo Okuni. Its inclusion in the music ensemble made kabuki even livelier, closer to the kind of kabuki that we can see today. This occurred around the Genroku period (1688–1704), a period which is famous as the first great flowering of Edo common culture.

CHIKAMATSU MONZAEMON—THE INTRODUCTION OF STORY LINES TO KABUKI

Kabuki plays were originally loose collections of song, dance and sketches. Complex storylines were first introduced into kabuki around the Genroku period. The pioneering playwright was Chikamatsu Monzaemon (1653–1724), whose plays are known around the world and who some call the "Japanese Shakespeare". Today we have television to report on current events, but at the beginning of the eighteenth century Chikamatsu took timely events of the day and quickly dramatized them. This was no easy task, since the shogunate strictly banned the depiction of contemporary events on stage, especially those concerning samurai, and so such events had to be set in the remote past, and all the names had to be changed, even if it was obvious what the play was about.

Chikamatsu was not only the first to dramatize the scandals of the commoners, he was also among the first to depict noteworthy incidents among the ruling class. The best known example of this genre is his rendition of the 1702 vendetta, called, in English, the Forty-Seven Ronin. Chikamatsu's classic version, *Kanadehon Chushingura* (The Treasury of Loyal Retainers), was written in 1748, nearly half a century after the actual event. But Chikamatsu had already dramatized it in the 1706 play *Goban Taiheiki* (The Go Board Chronicle), on which he later based *Kanadehon Chushingura*.

Soon after the Genroku period, scenes of everyday life were introduced into kabuki. These dramas were different from the lively rhythmical dances of early kabuki and Chikamatsu was instrumental in bringing them about.

Chikamatsu originally wrote for the bunraku puppet theater. There is a rich tradition of musical storytelling in Japan, and by the Edo period it had become a sophisticated literary and musical art, comprising narrative acted out by puppets. Chikamatsu was instrumental in raising the level of writing for the puppet theater, but it seems that he switched to writing for the kabuki theater as a result of a disagreement with the puppet theater people.

There are many plays in kabuki and the puppet theater with the same story lines, and that is for the simple reason that they were written by the same playwrights, of whom Chikamatsu was one of the most important. But even though the stories are the same, obviously the methods of presentation are quite different in the puppet theater and the live theater. One aspect of this is the freedom of mobility: puppets can easily go from the stage to the top balcony and down again. It is not nearly as easy for the human actors to change location in the kabuki theater. While puppets can simply be hauled about, an actor has to run upstairs, and it is necessary to cover the gap with music or some other diversion.

Today the immensely popular actor Ichikawa Ennosuke fills his kabuki productions with acrobatics and flights through the air. Even though many of these effects have their origins in the Edo period, probably under the influence of the puppet theater, his productions are often criticized. When other kabuki actors criticize these productions as being too circus-like, we can see the continuing strength of the idea that such effects should be left to the puppet theater.

DANJURO IN THE EAST; TOJURO IN THE WEST

In the Genroku period at the beginning of the eighteenth century, there were two great kabuki actors, Ichikawa Danjuro in Edo and Sakata Tojuro in Kamigata, that is, the region of Kyoto and Osaka. Edo and Kamigata have always had different cultures, Edo being a brash new town of samurai and Kamigata being a world of the old court nobility, established craftsmen, and properous merchants.

It is said that the first Ichikawa Danjuro was born in Edo around 1662, but the facts are not clear. The present Danjuro is the twelfth bearer of the name. Beginning with its founder, the Danjuro line has specialized in the type of expression called *aragoto*, which dramatizes the stories of warriors.

At the same time, in Kamigata, Sakata Tojuro was active. As opposed to Danjuro's *aragoto*, Tojuro took his material from daily life and, as a star actor, made popular the relatively realistic genre known as *sewamono*.

Chikamatsu had returned to writing for the puppet theater, and his realistic plots were drawing people to the puppets, away from kabuki. In particular, Chikamatsu's love suicide plays were sensationally popular.

Faced with the increasing popularity of the puppet theater, Danjuro I must have considered including realistic stories in his performances as well, but since the return of Chikamatsu to the puppet theater there was no comparable playwright for kabuki. Even if kabuki wanted to compete with the puppet theater the kabuki plays could not compare as stories of the real world. The lifeblood of Edo theater was still the superhuman and fabulous warrior heroes of the *aragoto* style and Danjuro must have decided then that he would have to continue with unrealistic, fantastic plays. The plays created once this decision was made, such as *Narukami* and *Shibaraku*, are still at the core of the *aragoto* repertory.

The heroic and bombastic movements of *aragoto* are far removed from reality. The *kumadori* makeup is also highly exaggerated. In all this there is nothing like the realism of the stories that Chikamatsu wrote for bunraku. But in this fictional fantastic world there is great dynamism, and Danjuro achieved great popularity and established the *aragoto* style in kabuki.

In Kamigata, Sakata Tojuro achieved success with the love suicide plays that Chikamatsu first made popular in the puppet theater. These were domestic plays that took their material from daily life as depicted in the scandal sheets of the time. However one looks at it, in life as in the theater, a recurring theme is the relations between men and women. The realistic plays of Tojuro that showed the complications of relationships between men and women, especially love triangles, captured the hearts of a large audience. Moreover, Tojuro largely performed in Osaka, a city of merchants. Stories dealing with human relationships and money struck at the core of the feelings of the people of Osaka.

In real life as well, Tojuro seems to have been quite a playboy. The portrait of Tojuro as a playboy in Kikuchi Kan's play *Tojuro no Koi* (The Love of Tojuro), written in 1919 and later made into a famous film, seems to be pretty close to the truth. In this play Tojuro makes the wife of a merchant believe that he is really in love with her and ends up destroying her life, all in order to observe the situation and enrich his own art.

The *sewamono* genre initiated by Tojuro with his search for realism continues to this day. In the nineteenth century Tojuro started to write about the lower classes of society, including plays with beggars and outcasts and thieves as their protagonists. Even though all of these characters were rather romanticised and puffed up theatrically, the word *sewa* can probably be seen as close to the English word "realism," since it is the genre of kabuki that brought everyday life onto the kabuki stage.

THE GRAND OLD MAN OF KABUKI'S MIDDLE YEARS: Tsuruya Namboku

During the Edo period kabuki had its good and bad times. One of the more prosperous times was the half century from 1750. During this period Tanuma Okitsugu was the most powerful man in the shogunate, leading a corrupt government based on bribery, but conversely also causing a flowering of cultural activity in Edo. This was the period when Sugita Gempaku translated the first anatomy textbook from Dutch into Japanese, when the Ukiyo-e woodblock print artist Suzuki Harunobu was active, and it was the time when sumo wrestling began to be run on a large scale.

There were bunraku playwrights such as Takeda Izumo II, one of the writers of *Kanadehon Chushingura*, Chikamatsu Hanji, one of the writers of *Honcho Nijushiko* (The Japanese Twenty-four Examples of Filial Piety), and kabuki playwright Tsuruya Namboku IV, whose works in particular led to a second golden age. Chikamatsu may have created *sewamono* for Kamigata with his poetic tales of the lives of commoners, but Namboku created *sewamono* for Edo, plays more graphic than realistic, eerily gruesome with a large dose of humor. His plays are fantastic and full of stage tricks, but they also sharply depict a kind of extreme psychology not explored by Chikamatsu.

Namboku's most famous play is *Tokaido Yotsuya Kaidan* (The Ghosts of Yotsuya). This play shows the underside of the world depicted in *Kanadehon Chushingura*. The protagonist is a masterless samurai named Tamiya Iemon who is one of the samurai rendered masterless by the death of their master. Even though he is one of the heroes of *Chushingura*, Iemon himself is a villain, callous and murderous on one hand, and a stylish and handsome man on the other. He is married and has a child. The young girl who lives next door, Oume, falls in love with Iemon the first time she sees him. Her grandfather is a wealthy doctor in the employ of Ko no Moronao, the villain and target of the vendetta in *Chushingura*. Despite the fact that Iemon loves his wife and, without her knowledge, killed her father to get her, the wealth and power of the young girl's family sway him. The doctor poisons and disfigures Iemon's wife to induce him to marry Oume. Iemon's wife, Oiwa, dies after a dramatic scene in which she vents her jealous fury, and her angry spirit forces Iemon to kill his new bride and her grandfather. In the end Oiwa's implacable, vengeful spirit triumphs. The play takes place within the framework of *Chushingura* but sardonically twists it around to reveal individual passion and greed.

The plays themselves were not the only factors in kabuki's success. It was also a great age for the creation of stage devices. For example, the playwright Namiki Shozo is credited with having invented the revolving stage in this period. This revolving stage was further developed by Hasegawa Kambei II who invented the *ja no me* or "snake's eye" stage, which complicated the device by splitting it into two concentric circles that could be used independently. So the revolving stage, which we tend to think of as a modern invention, has already been in use on the kabuki stage for two centuries.

The kabuki audience was not composed only of commoners, but also included the samurai class. Although the play itself was written much later, we have evidence of this in the play *Kiwametsuke Banzui Chobei* (Chobei Killed in the Bath). This play is about a famous Genroku period commoner who was a kind of Robin Hood figure. In the play we are shown samurai coming to see the kabuki theater and picking fights with the commoner audience.

Women were also an important part of the kabuki audience, as we know from the Ejima Incident of 1714, which involved a lady-in-waiting from the shogun's palace. The story indicates that even women of high station would slip out of the palace to see kabuki.

Danjuro VII, the Creator of *Kanjincho*

The histories of noh and kabuki are in many ways inseparable. One of the most famous kabuki plays to be based on a noh play is *Kanjincho*, which concerns the famous general Minamoto Yoshitsune who was fleeing from his brother Yoritomo, the shogun. Due to the cleverness of Yoshitsune's companion Benkei, who convinces the guards that they are genuine priests by pretending to read from a subscription list or *kanjincho*, a document enabling them to collect funds for the building of a temple, they manage to pass the barrier.

There were many previous plays about Yoshitsune and Benkei, but *Kanjincho* was unusual at the time since, even though it uses kabuki dance and *mie* poses, it was closely based on the original noh play. Around 1830, Ichikawa Danjuro VII (1791–1859), a descendent of the Danjuro that developed the *aragoto* style, managed to sneak a look at the noh play *Ataka* and used it to create the play *Kanjincho*. There are many stories about the obstacles that he had to overcome to obtain the material for this play.

It is difficult to imagine today, but in the Edo period kabuki actors were not permitted to see noh theater because the noh theater was patronized exclusively by the ruling samurai class. The rigid class system excluded actors so that there was no avenue open for them to be permitted to see anything as exalted as noh. No matter how much Danjuro may have wanted to see noh for artistic reasons, it could not be arranged easily.

Danjuro went to his patrons and asked them to find some way for him to see a noh performance. They agreed to try. The samurai class might have been at the top of the four-class system but after one hundred and thirty years of peace, many of them had fallen into extreme poverty.

The poverty of their sponsoring class could not have led to a pleasant lifestyle for the noh performers, so that when Danjuro's patrons came saying that Danjuro wished to see noh, it was difficult to refuse the inducements offered. At the same time it would violate the noh actor's sense of rank and propriety to allow Danjuro to see noh openly. After much agonizing the performer finally said, "I am going to rehearse now. I will not be able to tell if someone watches from the next room." The noh play was performed and Danjuro watched secretly from the next room. The play was *Ataka*, the story of Yoshitsune and his followers passing through the barrier at Ataka.

At first the influence of noh on *Kanjincho* was very strong. This can be seen in the costumes. As we can see from old woodblock prints, at first it was performed in the *hakama* trousers (rather like long culottes) which are worn in the noh theater even today. Danjuro IX (1838–1903) changed the costume to the present enormously wide *hakama*, called *oguchi hakama*, worn in today's kabuki version.

THE STATUS OF KABUKI ACTORS RISES AS A RESULT OF THE COMMAND PERFORMANCE FOR THE MEIJI EMPEROR

Danjuro IX was not only talented as an actor but he was also skilled as a promoter and he contributed greatly to raising the social status of kabuki actors. He had opportunities to do this after the Meiji Restoration brought an end to the Tokugawa government and its rigid four class system. In 1888, the twentieth year of the Meiji period, in the presence of the Meiji Emperor himself, Danjuro gave the first ever command performance of kabuki.

Kabuki was essentially entertainment for commoners and it would have been impossible for the emperor or high-ranking government ministers to go to see it. But as a result of the performance for the emperor, the attitude of the public toward kabuki and kabuki actors changed greatly. It even became acceptable for kabuki actors to be called *haiyu*, a polite word for actor, instead of *yakusha* which has rather pejorative connotations. No ordinary actor could have arranged for the emperor and the highest-ranking government ministers to gather to watch kabuki.

But Danjuro may have been too successful. Today it sometimes seems that kabuki has become too refined and lost its bonds with its audience. Some people accuse it of having become merely an amusement for rich people, or a place to hold meetings of couples for the arranged marriages amongst the elite. The problem of how kabuki is to relate to its audiences is something that we kabuki actors must think about very seriously.

Nonetheless, at the time Danjuro IX's imperial performance was a great success. One sign of this is the fact that two years later, in 1890, the Kabuki-za opened in Ginza. This was a new theater independent of the old three-theater system, and right in the middle of Tokyo, not in the outskirts to which the theaters had been banished in some of the Edo-period reforms. The capital for its construction was gathered quickly, while the political world was still impressed.

The first Kabuki-za was built, like the Imperial Theater built at about the same time, in the prestigious Western style. Although the theater was later rebuilt in a more appropriate traditional style, there has always been a problem with the size of the stage. About three-quarters of kabuki's repertory came originally from noh, and perhaps as a result of this, for most of its history the kabuki stage had been a widened version of the noh stage, even retaining its roof in some form.

The stage used for noh is 3-*ken* x 3-*ken*, in other words, a square space amounting to a little less than six square meters. In the Edo period approximately the same space was used for the main action on the kabuki stage, with a kind of forestage and an extension of the stage left, along with the *hanamichi* runway going through the audience. Today, the stage at the Kabuki-za is 14-*ken* wide or about twenty-five meters, about four times the size of the noh stage and appreciably bigger than the old kabuki stages.

When the stage gets this big even walking becomes a problem. The distance that could be covered in three steps now takes fourteen or fifteen. And if movements and gestures are not made larger they will not have any impact on such a large stage. Unavoidably, the art of kabuki has changed to fit this 14-*ken* stage.

The stage is not the only thing that changed. The stage that had always been in the half-darkness of candlelight is now lit up like high noon by electricity. Naturally this development affected the actors' costumes, which came to seem gaudy. In 1882, at the Shintomi-za, for the first time evening performances of kabuki were permitted. Before this time, for fear of fire among other things, nighttime performances had been forbidden.

As a result of the change in the physical conditions of kabuki, Meiji kabuki changed greatly from the kabuki of Izumo Okuni or the kabuki of the eighteenth century. Naturally, the acting changed as well. What once glimmered in the shadows of a candlelit theater now flashed and sparkled, and acting that once was designed to thrill and seduce a vulgar class became an entertainment for the new elite.

But there is another tradition as well. In the past, kabuki was not performed only in large luxurious theaters. Until World War II there were many small local theaters around Tokyo, and there various forms of kabuki were performed.

Some of these theaters were well appointed even if they were not considered as important as the Kabuki-za. Here, talented actors from lesser lineages could become stars. For example, at one theater inside a department store, the actor Kawarazaki Gonjuro could act the starring roles in the plays that belonged to the Ichikawa Danjuro lineage, and be such a hit that he could be called the Danjuro of the Toyoko Theater (*Toyoko no Ebizo*, Ebizo being one of the names in the Danjuro line). At the Kabuki-za, Gonjuro could never hope to play such roles. Today at the Kabuki-za he is one of the finest supporting actors in kabuki.

There were even more theaters that were not quite as large or handsome. Some of today's old movie theaters have a long history going back before World War II when, likely as not, they were live theaters.

I live in Yokohama where there is a movie theater and popular theater called the Sugita Gekijo. Right after the war, the late Hakuo and his son, the present Matsumoto Koshiro performed kabuki there. I never saw this myself, but my mother-in-law remembers going often. Thus, even though this theater had become a movie theater, live theater continued to be performed there as well.

As a boy I lived in the rural outskirts of Tokyo and on a street near where I lived there is a movie theater called the Gekko-kan. It was always there, and I remember that even though it was such an out of the way place they used to perform theater there as well. At the time many movie theaters had double bills, with one movie and one show. Kabuki was the main attraction, not the film. There must have been many such theaters with programs aimed at ordinary people.

Before the war, then, it was easy to go see kabuki either at a grand theater like the Kabuki-za, or at one of the many small theaters.

That this popular kabuki gradually separated from its mass audience is due partly to the power of the production company. Shochiku has continually worked to preserve kabuki and is responsible for the fact that it exists today. While I am very thankful for that, in some ways Shochiku's management of kabuki and the way that they have had to preserve it has been a mixed blessing. In the Taisho period (1912–1926), Shochiku began its move to hold all kabuki actors under exclusive contract. There have been many benefits from this system, but it has also been one major cause of the change in kabuki from a popular art form into the kind of elegant pastime for rich connoisseurs that it seems to have become today.

One group of kabuki actors that opposed Shochiku's policies and the oppressing *iemoto* system broke away from Shochiku in 1931 to form what is now Zenshin-za. To this day Zenshin-za remains independent, performing both modern, leftist drama and kabuki. A little earlier, in 1930, the late actors Chusha and Kodayu led a group of leftist actors to form the Taishu-za or "Popular Theater."

During the war, performances of kabuki were stopped briefly, but after the war was over, production was resumed. The Kabuki-za was damaged, but in 1951 it was rebuilt on an even grander scale than before. By this time, nearly all kabuki actors had contracts with Shochiku and kabuki continued on the path that led away from the prewar system of kabuki playing in both small popular theaters as well as the larger theaters for elite audiences.

CHAPTER 2

The *Iemoto* System

The backstage of a kabuki theater reveals a world where all the artists and craftsmen have a very firm idea of where they belong. The setup of the dressing rooms, who serves whom, and where people sit, directly reflect the inner social system that preserves kabuki today, something that is often described as the "*iemoto* system." Kabuki and other traditional art forms like classical dance, traditional music and tea ceremony are organized along the lines of the *iemoto* system. In fact, the world of classical dance overlaps with kabuki since most of the its repertory originated in the kabuki theater and some kabuki actors are the heads of branches of schools of dance.

Under the *iemoto* system dancers of a particular school, or actors of a particular family, or practitioners of the tea ceremony are given artistic names and receive permission from the head of the group, or *iemoto*, to practice the art. The *iemoto* thus has control both over who will be allowed within the group and what will be done within it. In kabuki this means that it is the heads of important acting families who largely control the art. These actors are our elders (*senpai*) and teachers, and they control who can become a kabuki actor, how far an actor can advance and what can be allowed on stage.

At times this system has been strongly criticized as being feudal or outdated, since it seems to restrict career entrance and advancement, and many think that it stifles creativity. But the existence of this system is one reason that kabuki has been preserved. If one constantly performed new works and revised existing works according to a variety of new interpretations, there would be hundreds of new pieces, most of which would probably vanish without a trace. The noh repertory and kabuki artistic traditions have been preserved and refined by the *iemoto* system for, respectively, six hundred and four hundred years.

Despite this, I cannot say that I am totally in agreement with the *iemoto* system as it exists today. The problem is very complicated, and includes the question of whether kabuki will have the flexibility to change and develop as an art form to entertain and move contemporary audiences. It also includes the question of where the kabuki actors of the future will come from and what kind of social organization they will join to both confine and support them.

Kabuki's greatness lies in its tradition of acting. But theater does not exist without an audience and to keep an art form alive, there are times when it is harmful to cling to antiquated practices. For instance, when I perform abroad, there are many times when I need to be flexible and it would be encouraging to think that important kabuki actors could overlook certain breaches of tradition.

When an audience with absolutely no prior knowledge of kabuki encounters the real thing they are not likely to understand it at all. One act of a kabuki play usually lasts a good hour, rather too much for an audience used to the pace of television. So for audiences abroad, we often just perform the essence of a scene. I often use the piece *Funa Benkei* (Benkei in the Boat) on these occasions. In the first half, Shizuka Gozen, the lover of general Yoshitsune who is fleeing into exile, dances her farewell to him. Since this is a female character, it is an *onnagata* dance. In the second half there is a dance by the ghost of Taira no Tomomori, a rival general whose entire clan was defeated by Yoshitsune in a sea battle. Performing both halves takes more time than is usually available so we usually present just an excerpt of either Shizuka's dance or Tomomori's dance in a kabuki demonstration.

Of course, this chops up *Funa Benkei* and does not leave it in its original form. Even though today it is usual to present only certain parts of long full-length plays, a single act is kept more or less intact, especially in the case of a play like *Funa Benkei*, which is taken straight from noh and is complete in one act. Breaching tradition by abbreviating plays in this way would undoubtedly make the senior kabuki actors extremely unhappy. They would probably declare that this was not *Funa Benkei* at all, and that it drained the play of all its meaning.

There are those who believe that art does not need explanation, and senior kabuki actors almost certainly believe that the most important thing is to present perfectly polished art without extraneous chatter. This is the way to transmit the essence of the art. But I believe that in order to teach kabuki to young people today, and even more so, in order to teach kabuki to people abroad, it is necessary to explain what is going on.

For such people, an encounter with kabuki uncut and unexplained may leave them just as uninformed as before. In fact, on occasion not only will they not understand the performance, but they may find it painful. At the beginning, to foster understanding, it is necessary to condense kabuki a little.

This is true not only for audiences but for the actors in training as well, and for Japanese and non-Japanese. The young Japanese students in the National Theater training program shower me with exactly the same questions as American students at the University of Hawaii. It has become difficult to teach kabuki to young, highly Westernized Japanese in their twenties. One can no longer expect an instant meeting of hearts. No matter how much it may infuriate senior kabuki actors, I believe that we simply have no choice but to cut things down for teaching.

TRAINING

Teaching kabuki to create a new generation of actors is becoming increasingly important. The most important distinction between actors is between the descendants of major acting families, and actors who come from outside these families. In the old days, someone who wanted to become a kabuki actor apprenticed himself to a major actor. He would do odd jobs and learn by watching. People can still enter the theater world this way, but there is not nearly enough kabuki performed today to learn just by watching and there are not enough apprentices to ensure that there will be enough actors to perform kabuki in the future. This is the reason a training program was established at the National Theater to supplement traditional methods.

The National Theater training program was begun in 1970 by Bando Mitsugoro, the late Ichikawa Sadanji, and Nakamura Matagoro, and is under the supervision of the Bunka-cho (Ministry of Culture). The course of study is two years, and only about ten students can be accepted every two years. Class sizes must be kept small for the exacting training in dance, music, fight movements, and for the scenes that are used to teach kabuki. Moreover, the kabuki world can only absorb so many new actors at a time. From the beginning, the head of the training program has been my own teacher, Nakamura Matagoro II, and I have assisted Matagoro as an instructor.

We have found that the biggest problem is in placing the students once the two-year training program is completed. In March 1972 our first group of students demonstrated the skills that they had learned in a graduation recital at the conclusion of two years of hard work. But even though they had completed the program, they were by no means ready to play starring roles on major kabuki stages, and those of us responsible for the program had no idea what to do with these young kabuki actors of the future.

The National Theater of Japan has a splendid building with three theaters, precious rehearsal space, and an archive, but does not maintain its own troupe of kabuki actors. The Moscow Art Theater is under the protection of the government and has both a theater and a troupe of actors so that it can put performances on by itself. The same is true for the Royal Shakespeare Company. However, while the Japanese National Theater has a theater, and even trains actors, it offers no opportunity for regular employment in its own troupe.

How are stars trained? Up until now in the kabuki world, few people have had access to training by senior actors and teachers of music and dance unless they were already related somehow. This is because by and large succession is passed down from father to one child. For example, the name of Danjuro is the most important in the Ichikawa family and the holder of this name is essentially the *iemoto* of the Ichikawa acting family. One Danjuro would pass on his acting skills to his son, then eventually that son would take the name of Danjuro as well. This is how names like Danjuro and Utaemon—two of the most powerful names in the kabuki world—are passed down from generation to generation.

A younger actor not of the direct *iemoto* line, will generally not have the opportunity to learn an important role directly from a senior actor who has mastered it. The only way to for him to learn is to watch the senior actors' performances and "steal" from that. Of course, kabuki training places great emphasis on learning to memorize what another actor does and to be able to reproduce it quickly and accurately. But getting individual direction from a teacher and hearing about the fine details of a role from a master actor who has polished his performance through years of experience makes all the difference. This kind of training is only granted to an elite, because they are the only actors who will conceivably have the opportunity to perform the great starring roles.

But kabuki will strangle itself if it only concerns itself with the training of stars. There are heirs to follow in the line of major actors, but there are few supporting actors left. The major actors, who are known as *onadai*, or "major" *nadai* actors, have mostly concentrated on educating their immediate successors, that is, their own sons and adopted heirs. They have not paid much attention to other unrelated young actors.

A big star cannot put on a play by himself. He needs major supporting actors: experienced actors in minor roles who are vital to creating the kabuki atmosphere and large crowds of bit actors to play ladies-in-waiting, maids, geisha, porters, firemen, sumo wrestlers and soldiers. A kabuki hero cannot act heroic without a crowd of actors trained in the flips and actobatics that make up the dance-like *tachimawari* fight scenes. In the play *Benten Kozo* (Benten the Thief) there is a spectacular final scene where Benten is arrested. This takes place on the roof of a temple and for the big fight scene or *tachimawari*, some twenty people are needed to shout, "You're under arrest!" before they go through the precisely choreographed fight movements with Benten. The star playing Benten mimes his blows and poses dramatically while the other actors do the acrobatics. But there are never enough actors to play these arresting officials. This is because the roles of these officers, or *torite* are played by *nadai-shita* actors, that is actors that have not reached the rank of *nadai*, and there are no longer enough *nadai-shita* actors to cast these scenes easily.

One might think that the numbers could be made up by having ranking *nadai* actors help out, but that would not do either. Unlike Peking Opera, where acrobatic movements are important for stars as well, in kabuki the star's job is to pose dramatically and not endanger himself by performing acrobatics. In the kabuki heirarchy, there is a strict tradition that *torite* are only played by *nadai-shita* actors. In order for kabuki to continue it is necessary to train such supporting actors. The training program at the National Theater was born to meet that need.

Before the training program was created, people became kabuki actors by becoming the apprentices or *deshi* of major kabuki actors. This path has the advantage that one is a professional from the start instead of being a student for two years.

Our first students knew nothing about kabuki, but after two years of contact with the kabuki world at close quarters, they came to learn just how grueling it is to be a *deshi* within the *iemoto* system. For better or worse, they had come to know the inner workings of the kabuki world and so were set against becoming *deshi*.

On the other hand, kabuki actors always want *deshi*. This is because it is impossible to perform kabuki without them. For example, the story of *Benten Kozo* is the story of five thieves under the leadership of Nippon Daemon. These five thieves are always played by top kabuki actors. But without *deshi* or arresting officers to fight with, even the best kabuki actor cannot make an impressive thief.

When our first group of students finished their training, aggressive scouting by kabuki actors began. The students did not want to become *deshi* if they could avoid it, but the established kabuki actors were very insistent. Since there were only ten students, they were in great demand.

As head of the program, Matagoro felt a sense of responsibility for the students. He was concerned about the intensity of the scouting from the kabuki world and worried about whether this was the best solution for our students. I was concerned as well and tried to take matters into my own hands. Filled with a sense of righteous indignation I went to the Bunka-cho. It seemed ridiculous to me that the National Theater could not support its own theater troupe and so I went and insisted that our students should be taken in by the National Theater and that a theater troupe like the Royal Shakespeare Company should be established, instead of placing our students in the established kabuki world as *deshi*. My visit created quite a stir, which shows what a sensitive issue this is. Nevertheless, Matagoro and the other teachers in charge of the program decided that the best existing solution, although imperfect, was to have our students continue their training and to find their position in the kabuki world as *deshi* of major actors.

I am not sure that this is the best solution. To be blunt, the problem is the way the *iemoto* system constricts the kabuki world; this is the great limitation of the *iemoto* system. From 1973, when the National Theater training program began, to the present, there has not been a single example of someone from outside the group of *onadai* actors becoming a star. They cannot get starring roles. Only *onadai* can make it to the top.

Of course there are some exceptions. There is a young actor named Ichikawa Emiya who was a member of the fourth group of students in the National Theater training program who has now won the strong support of Ichikawa Ennosuke. Ennosuke has created a huge new audience for kabuki, but his kabuki is somewhat different from that of the established kabuki world. In order to perform his plays he has had to assemble his own group of actors, and this also gives him the freedom to support talented young actors. Emiya is a rare example of a talented young actor from outside of the kabuki world who has been given the opportunity to play starring roles. This experience is precious because an *onnagata* may have lessons in dance and music but unless he has the opportunity to perform on stage with a talented actor, he cannot add depth and subtlety to his acting. Emiya has great talent, but it is Ennosuke's patronage that has allowed him to play good roles.

There are still many obstacles that Emiya will run up against before he can become a kabuki star. That is because becoming a kabuki star is not simply a matter of individual talent and ability;

Emiya is not yet in a position to get good roles simply on the basis of his own talent. This is true for all actors—the roles they can get are determined more by family and connections than talent.

In the plays of the Kabuki Juhachiban collection, that is, the classic plays of the Ichikawa family like *Shibaraku* and *Kanjincho,* which actor can play which role is almost totally fixed. For an actor like myself who has come from outside the kabuki world, the chances are nearly non-existent to ever play a starring role in one of these plays on a major kabuki stage.

But one cannot say that if kabuki gets rid of the *iemoto* system, and goes purely on ability, actors better than the ones on stage today will emerge. On the contrary, in that case kabuki would probably be unable to continue. The family system still has the capacity to create actors with abilities that are different from the skills that talented actors can develop with even the best training.

That children of *onadai* may possess abilities ordinary people do not have is is not surprising, because since birth they have breathed the air of the kabuki world as though it were the most natural thing in the world. In the same way that Japanese children born in America can speak English better than Japanese professors of English, these heirs to the kabuki world have the strength of being born actors. I have seen how much these young heirs differ from ordinary people with my own eyes time after time. Take Matsumoto Koshiro IX, the oldest son of Matsumoto Koshiro VIII, for example. When I first encountered him, he was fourteen or fifteen and had the name Ichikawa Somegoro. But even at a glance one could see that there was something different about this boy. It is difficult to put into words, but like a race horse of good breeding his poise and physical appearance showed that he was a thoroughbred from a distinguished line of actors. The difference is more profound than simply a difference in individual talent or ability.

Somegoro's father had already achieved the rank of the name Matsumoto Koshiro VIII. To trace this family's origins, you'd have to go all the way back to 1730, just before kabuki's second flowering, when Namiki Shozo was writing plays. Koshiro's acting thus has two hundred years of experience behind it, experience that has created the acting traits that are carefully copied and transmitted through the generations of the Matsumoto family. The individual talent and experience of a solitary actor cannot possibly match the weight of this kind of history.

It may be disrespectful to Koshiro to try to measure this in terms of money, but just think of what is spent on publicity. For two hundred years there has been an actor named Matsumoto Koshiro. In that two hundred years, the money spent publicizing the name would amount to quite a fortune. If you took the name Ichikawa Danjuro, which since 1760 has been printed and handwritten on all kinds of things, you would find that an incalculable fortune has been invested in this tradition.

This is part of the strength of tradition. Even if I had unlimited wealth to publicize my career and to invest in making the name Nakamura Matazo famous, time would defeat me. There is no way to match my thirty years on stage against a process that has continued for over two hundred years.

The same is true for Ichikawa Emiya. His chance came with a starring role in Ennosuke's new kabuki play about the ancient Japanese hero Yamato Takeru. Emiya is wonderful as an *onnagata*, but the time and money that has been and will be spent on polishing his artistic skills is nothing compared to that spent on the real stars of the play, established actors like Ichikawa Ennosuke or Nakamura Tokizo. A family line that has been nourished by history creates actors with all kinds of tangible and intangible qualities that cannot be acquired through education. These qualities are worth a great deal. Perhaps they are the real value of kabuki.

It is important to remember that it is the famous families that have nourished and supported kabuki to the present day. We cannot discard them. But it is also true that if we simply depend on tradition and those *iemoto*, kabuki will disappear. As I said before, we are now facing a time when supporting actors are extremely scarce. Moreover, we are faced with a threatening situation inasmuch as the general public is losing interest in kabuki and it is appreciated by only a small group of rich people.

Of course, catering to a rich audience brings more profits for the production company. But if things continue this way, kabuki may lose its audience entirely. This cannot have been what Danjuro IX intended when he raised the status of kabuki in the Meiji period. Nor can he have been aiming at making kabuki actors a rich, arrogant elite. Up until the Meiji period actors were regarded as distinctly lower class, and he must have simply wanted actors to receive at least the same respect as greengrocers and fishmongers. He went to great lengths to arrange for a peformance before the emperor simply so that the existence of kabuki could be publicly acknowledged. This is also why he worked to produce new historical plays that would be acceptable to new tastes in realism and education.

Danjuro IX's goals may have been modest, but today the adverse effects of his work are all too apparent. Perhaps kabuki has been made too precious, putting it out of reach of the public, and making it instead an entertainment for a small number of rich people, supplemented by large groups of others, who receive their tickets from a company or some other organization and attend out of a sense of social obligation. In fact it often seems that the primary interest of many kabuki-goers today lies in something other than the kabuki performance itself. This is not a healthy situation.

We need to find a middle way for kabuki today, incorporating its earlier dramatic vitality with the social acceptance Danjuro IX gained for it. Danjuro IX might be surprised to see the kabuki productions of Ichikawa Ennosuke, which are full of fast costume changes, stage tricks, and other devices to thrill a mass audience. Many of his contemporaries accuse Ennosuke of vulgarizing the classical art of kabuki and turning it into a circus. Yet, leaving aside the finer artistic points, what Ennosuke is attempting is of great importance to the survival of kabuki—to bring back into the theater people who love kabuki.

For kabuki as a whole to attract such an audience we need to make certain adaptations. One, which has proved succesful abroad, is to perform condensed versions of classic plays from the Danjuro repertoire, such as *Kanjincho*. While such an innovation might outrage today's senior actors, an understanding of the motivation might convince them that, in a universal art like theater, changes can be made out of respect for traditions and a longing to keep them alive. Kabuki now has an international audience, and experiments such as the kabuki workshop described in the last chapter of this book may prove to be what is needed to introduce it to new audiences all around the world.

CHAPTER 3

An Actor's Story

Kabuki is usually considered a world sealed off, a world that is not entered unless one is born into an acting family with centuries of tradition behind it. My family had no connection to kabuki whatsoever. I born into a family that made and sold *konnyaku*, a jelly made from yam starch and used in Japanese cooking. How did this *konnyaku* maker's son with no connection to the performing arts enter the closed traditional world of kabuki?

It just somehow happened. This is true, but saying it so simply might offend my elders in the kabuki world. There were many stages to the process but it started with a meeting with a remarkable man. It was an encounter with a kabuki actor, the late Bando Mitsugoro VIII (1906–1975), that changed my life. He was an immensely cultured man who was well known as a Japanese dancer and as the author of many books of essays. A great gourmet as well, Mitsugoro died tragically after eating the poisonous blowfish *fugu*, a delicacy that can be fatal if not properly prepared.

I first became interested in theater in high school, but I didn't even think of performing kabuki until I was in college—way too late to begin by all kabuki conventional wisdom.

In the traditional performing arts there is a belief that the most auspicious time to begin training is the sixth day of the sixth month of one's sixth year. This is not just superstition, because for kabuki in particular that early training is crucial; what is learned at that age is never forgotten. As a rule, students of traditional arts are taught to imitate the teacher without any explanations. Young children are especially receptive to this kind of training, and get a solid training in the fundamentals without having to think about it, absorbing it all naturally.

From this point of view, I've only had a half portion of the tradition of kabuki since I didn't start my training until I reached "middle age." I know *Kanjincho*, but that is because I studied it by watching intently and memorizing it as an adult. My *Kanjincho* is somehow different from that of the child in a kabuki family who learned it without special effort, growing into it by playing the different roles through his career.

The same is true for other skills related to kabuki. Music and dance are the foundation of kabuki movement and acting. If one can play the *shamisen* and the *taiko* stick drum, but cannot play the *kotsuzumi* hand drum, then something is missing in one's acting. In kabuki, much depends on sensitive coordination of movement and music. My teacher, Nakamura Matagoro, knows a vast amount about kabuki music, knowledge accumulated over some sixty years of experience on stage. An actor like me who started in his twenties can't even hope to compete.

FROM WARTIME TO HIGH SCHOOL THEATRICALS

At the age at which a kabuki actor would already be in training, I was not even interested in theater. But other early experiences were important and, in a strange way, led to what I am doing now. In the sixth month of *my* sixth year, Japan was at war with China. It was no time for theater. My father ran a *konnyaku* business in Musashi Koyama in Tokyo. In 1943 we were evacuated out of the city to his native Yamagata prefecture to escape the bombing.

As a Tokyo boy who could not speak the distinctive Tohoku dialect I had a rough time, since I was constantly the target of the local children's bullying. I had to work at hard physical labor of a sort that city children didn't experience, cutting grass, making straw sandals, drawing pails of water and carrying tubs of human waste for fertilizer. But in a way, I was fortunate to have had this experience because much later it turned out to be useful on the kabuki stage.

When the war ended my father took us back to Tokyo, which was now a burnt wasteland, and immediately returned to his prewar craft of making and selling *konnyaku*. My older sister and I would go together with my father to the Musashi Koyama train station near our home to sell the *konnyaku*.

This was the first time in my life that I had gone out to sell anything. In Japan, food sellers bellow out calls to greet and attract a customers. But I was timid and couldn't bring myself to shout "Come and buy!" Try as I might, I could only get out a voice about as big as the buzzing of a mosquito. Astonishingly enough, in 1962 I received a prize for my recording of *Kiyari-uta*, a kind of boisterous work song. Perhaps this shows that I have the same blood as my vociferous father and sister after all. With their energetic cries of "Freshly made *konnyaku!* How about some for your husband's supper?" our cartful of *konnyaku* was emptied in no time.

Later, even though the war had ended, there were few people who could speak English around Musashi Koyama. My sister was unusual in being able to do so, and, probably sent by our neighbors, American GIs would visit our house and ask for directions to the local bars and restaurants.

To me, the sudden appearances of these GIs were terrifying. War propaganda had made me afraid of them, and they were so tall that they loomed over me like giants. However, these giants would often leave gifts such as chocolate, chewing gum or cigarettes in return for getting directions.

This was how I first ate corned beef, and I thought it was delicious. I couldn't forget the taste and wanted more. But when I tried to say "Give me corned beef, please," to a GI in the English I had learned from my sister, perhaps because my pronunciation was bad, I got chocolate instead. This was my first attempt at English conversation and, angry and embarrassed, I was left standing there holding the chocolate.

I believe that to some extent this humiliating experience may be the source of my motivation for learning English. Now I can even give lectures and workshops to Americans and Europeans. Just like artistic training begun on the sixth day of the sixth month of one's sixth year, early life experiences are not easily forgotten either.

FROM SCHOLAR TO AMATEUR STAR IN HIGH SCHOOL

In 1946 I started middle school and for the next three years, even if I do say so myself, studied rather successfully. My father had not gone to school and was never happy with his difficulties with writing. He would always say, "If I had gone to school, I'd be the head of the *konnyaku* makers' association by now." These words kept me at my desk. My grades had been good since elementary school, so like all Japanese parents, my mother and my father dreamed that I might go to the top university in Japan, Tokyo University, and may be even get one of the most desired elite jobs, a position at the Ministry of Finance.

I worked hard to live up to my parents' expectations. Under the influence of my older brother and sister, I studied a good deal of English and struggled with it thinking that somehow I would eventually learn to enjoy it. My brother, who was slightly older than I, had an English storybook, *Robin Hood*, that was quite fancy for the time, and I remember pulling it off my brother's bookshelf to look at its brightly colored pictures.

In 1949 I entered Waseda Teijisei High School, an elite high school attached to Waseda University, which is famous for both its theater studies and amateur theatricals. Following my parents' wishes, I planned to go on to college, and almost as a matter of course, was aiming for Tokyo University, the university most difficult to enter in Japan.

I first saw stage shows during my time at high school, and Waseda University was full of student theater groups like the Free Stage and the Shakespeare Theater Troupe. Every week there was a performance somewhere on campus. The performance that I remember most intensely was Shakespeare's *Taming of the Shrew*. I was attracted to the theme of taming women since I had just begun being interested in girls myself. I watched plays, but at that time hadn't the slightest thought of going on stage.

I had gone to a lot of trouble to get into the Waseda-affiliated high school, but the political activity on campus then meant it was not an atmosphere in which to study for college entrance exams. We couldn't even study in the classrooms because activists would come and force the students to go with them to Okuma

Hall, the big auditorium on campus. At this rate I could never pass the entrance for into Tokyo University, so I talked things over with my mother and in the spring of 1950 transferred to another high school where things were quieter.

It is ironic that this transfer intended to help get me into Tokyo University awakened my passion for theater instead, and set me on the path to a career as an actor. At my new school, unexpectedly, I had to appear in an English-language drama and play the ghost of the late king in *Hamlet*.

This was my first appearance on stage. I was overwhelmed when my teacher praised me for my first lines on stage in English. I could finally forget the humiliation of the time I had tried to say, "Give me corned beef," all those years ago.

Moreover, it made me popular with the female students. I enjoyed this situation and the theater bug bit me. From that time on I began spending my spare time doing nothing but watching movies and English-language dramas. I ended up founding a drama club and became its president.

We put on plays like Osanai Kaoru's *Chichi Kaeru* (Father Returns) and plays written by the students. Looking back on it now, since we were completely self-taught, the productions could not have been very good. By that time I had seen a lot of movies and theater, and somehow, the plays got put on. In this way I was passionately involved with theater until I graduated from high school.

AN ENCOUNTER WITH NOH-STYLE DANCE

In my youthful exuberance I had begun to think of myself as an expert in amateur theater, and it came as a great shock when I encountered real theater. Kanze Fumihiko, a noh performer of the Kanze school, entered my high school. At the school festival he danced a noh *shimai*, the dance performed at the climax of a noh play which is often performed at amateur recitals and also on casual occasions. The amateur drama I knew simply could not compare with this. With his modern hairstyle, Kanze Fumihiko wore long *hakama* and danced the formal, classical movements of noh. I was dumfounded by his sense of style, especially since he was still just a student.

Suddenly my success with the drama club and the praise

received from my language teachers seemed less significant, and I now noticed that they had not actually praised my acting.I couldn't help being impressed by the dancing of Kanze, and started spending time with him. We even played *go*, a form of Japanese chess, despite the fact that I didn't really know the game. I asked him a lot of questions about the noh theater. I really would have liked him to give me lessons in noh, but was too proud at the time to bow my head before a younger student. My stupid pride made me lose a great opportunity.

Until then I had no particular interest in traditional performing arts like noh and kabuki. I was possessed by the movies. My high school was in Ginza, and every day I walked by the Kabuki-za on my way home from school. Even so I never went in, but walked past and went on to the movie theater nearby. I did not think that kabuki could offer me anything new. Besides, movies were cheaper so they were all I watched. I dreamed of becoming a movie director if I could.

As I concentrated more and more on theater and movies, naturally enough, I paid less attention to my studies. When I took the all-important entrance exam for Tokyo University, I was a spectacular failure. I spent a year as a *ronin*, a student who has failed his entrance exam and studies hard for another chance. I studied idly for the exam, my thoughts filled with the theater. Finally in 1952 I got into the literature department of Sophia University.

COLLEGE THEATER

Even though I had finally managed, only just, to enter college, I had no sooner started my studies than the theater bug bit again. I heard that the drama club was looking for members and joined, keeping it secret from my mother. By this time theater had entered my bloodstream.

Appropriately enough for a Catholic university, we performed the plays of T.S. Eliot, *Murder in the Cathedral* and *The Cocktail Party*, in translations by Fukuda Tsuneari. When we went to him for permission to perform the translated plays he offered to come and direct, so we learned the meaning of the plays from an expert. Through this drama club I came to know people like the playwright and popular novelist Inoue Hisashi, who is known in the West for his virtuouso one-woman play *Kesho* (Makeup) about a woman heading a troupe in the declining old-fashioned popular theater, and the German literature scholar, Kurahara Koreharu. Another fellow student was Isoura Koji who is now an announcer with the national television station NHK. I grew especially close to Isoura. He lived close to the Sophia campus and I visited him regularly.

It was Isoura who introduced me to the distinguished playwright Iizawa Tadasu. Even today, in his eighties, Iizawa is still writing his intelligent satires and comedies. He is one of the very few playwrights in Japan distinguished by being made a member of the Academy of Arts. Even though he works in modern theater, he knows and has worked with people throughout the theater world, traditional and modern, and has even written modern Kyogen-style plays and a kabuki dance.

Meeting Iizawa drew me even deeper into the theater world. I'm embarrassed to say this, but even though I was involved in theater, I at first had no idea who Iizawa Tadasu was. Isoura only told me that he was a playwright and arranged for me to meet him. The first thing Iizawa said when he saw me was, "You have a big face so you'd make a good kabuki actor." He also said, "You don't speak with any regional accent. If only you were taller you could be in movies." I was put off by his directness, but Isoura may have told him that I wanted to become an actor. As I listened to him he struck me as an extraordinary man. In particular, I was surprised at how he would speak openly about sex without ever seeming coarse.

I had never even considered becoming involved with kabuki, but after listening to Iizawa I set out on a path that would lead me to my teachers, the late Bando Mitsugoro and Nakamura Matagoro, and my decision to become a kabuki actor. It was also his introductions that helped smooth the way for me to enter the production company Toho.

Another former Sophia student who influenced my life was the talented Ishikawa Tangetsu, who wrote lyrics for Japanese traditional music and won the Arts Festival Prize for his *Kurisuto Dojoji* (Christian Dojoji). He would often come by his alma mater and give encouragement to the drama club. He ran a bar in Ginza and since we students had no money he often treated us to drinks.

Meeting My Future Teacher, Mitsugoro

In the winter of my second year at college, Ishikawa introduced me to the kabuki actor Bando Mitsugoro, then named Bando Minosuke, who was even then famous as a master of kabuki dance. I will never forget that occasion. It was on the second floor of an eel restaurant in Ueno named Izuei, a restaurant that has been serving eel dishes since the Edo period. It's still there in a big modern building, but then it was a just a tiny, elegantly constructed place.

In the room were Mitsugoro, Ishikawa, and I, just the three of us. Somehow I had this famous kabuki actor for company. Although there was a pot of *oden*, a kind of Japanese stew of fishcakes and various vegetables including *konnyaku*, boiling appetizingly in front of me, I was so nervous that I couldn't even reach out to take any. Mitsugoro encouraged me to eat, but by this time my legs had gone numb and I couldn't move. That was how tense I was.

Mitsugoro and Ishikawa nibbled on pieces of *oden* and talked passionately about theater. I could understand almost nothing of what they were saying. I only knew a word here and there of the technical vocabulary of kabuki and was only familiar with a few of the names of actors. This was not surprising since I had seen hardly any kabuki up to this time. All I could do was to sit silent and respectful in a corner of the room.

I kept quiet but I wasn't bored. It was like watching theater. As Mitsugoro chatted, somehow even his movements were different from those of other people. His timing was superb, and it was like watching a good play. Even just chatting about everyday matters, every position of his body was like a picture.

Mitsugoro's voice was quite loud. He was not trying to shout us down but simply had a voice that projected wery well. He laughed often in a pleasant tenor voice. I was completely captivated by his style, the richness of his conversation, the depth of his culture and how sharp he looked in kimono.

After I had finally relaxed a bit, Mitsugoro asked, "So, how did you get interested in kabuki?" Frankly, at that time I hadn't

even begun thinking about becoming an actor. I have no idea
how I answered the question. It seems that Mitsugoro thought
that we were being introduced because I had firm ambitions of
becoming a kabuki actor.

He gave me a lot of advice about becoming a kabuki actor that
went something like the following:

> Familiarize yourself with the classics. First, go watch the
> noh theater. Have you ever seen the bunraku puppet the-
> ater? You're going to have to learn to sing *gidayu*. That will
> train you to sing and to speak. Voice comes first, then move-
> ment, and then figure and bearing. An actor first has to
> train his voice. Poise and bearing can come third. For that you
> should study tea ceremony. If you take lessons in tea you
> will learn how to walk well. Do and you ever go to art muse-
> ums? Go and look at Buddhist sculptures from the Kama-
> kura period (1185–1333). Their *koshi* (hips) are set just
> right!

Mitsugoro was a magically persuasive speaker. He could talk
in a way that completely charmed me into being determined to
begin training as a kabuki actor.

Mitsugoro was different from any person that I had encountered before. He wore his kimono differently. Of course
the kimono itself was different in material and cut from that of
ordinary people, but more importantly, he wore it differently,
loosely, with an air of casual elegance. He wore his kimono long
enough to hide his heels. Also, I thought that usually people
who wore kimono should wear formal white *tabi* divided socks,
instead, Mitsugoro wore everyday black *tabi*.

The range of his knowledge was staggering. He moved easily
from talk of pictures to Buddhist sculpture to tea ceremony
without ever running out of things to say. I could keep up with
Iizawa's conversation since he spoke about Western things that
I was familiar with, but Mitsugoro left me speechless.

Mitsugoro talked about the Japanese classics, noh theater,
bunraku, and kabuki. Since I hadn't studied any of this I kept
feeling totally inadequate. In particular, he kept referring to the
poetry anthologies, *Kokinshu* and the *Shin Kokinshu*, pointing
out one work after another that was based on a particular poem

from the *Shin Kokinshu,* and quoting the poem from memory "I'm sure that you know the *Hyaku-nin Isshu.* Recite some of the poems that you know from it." This revealed my ignorance, for although I had studied the collection of poems for my entrance exams, suddenly asked in this fashion, I could only gape.

As soon as I got home, I started leafing through the *Kokinshu* and the *Shin Kokinshu.* I gradually learned that most noh plays are expansions on poems from the *Shin Kokinshu,* so that if you don't know the *Shin Kokinshu* then you can't understand noh or kabuki. Mitsugoro opened my eyes to the world of the Japanese classics.

After meeting Mitsugoro, I started thinking vaguely that I might like to try kabuki. Despite all his encouragement though, I did not immediately put the thought into practice, and wasted time with all sorts of other things. It was disrespectful to my teacher Mitsugoro and a terrible waste of time. Perhaps it was due to my youth. I didn't start serious kabuki training until after I graduated.

But this doesn't mean that I didn't want to study traditional performing arts. Together with Ishikawa, we began a study group called the Saikagi Juku (Cultivating Flower Art School). Despite its name, it was not a group to study flower arranging or sewing, it was a group to polish performing skills, in other words, a school for dance and *shamisen.* Ishikawa flattered me into studying traditional performance arts at the same time that I was in the drama club at Sophia performing Western plays.

T.S. Eliot didn't fit with Japanese classical dance and *shamisen* very well, but I wanted to try anything I found interesting. Because Ishikawa wrote texts for kabuki dance, he wanted to try having his own works performed. But he couldn't do that by himself, he needed the support of a group of trained performers. As the two of us discussed our plans, we decided to go ahead and try to build a troupe by organizing the necessary training ourselves.

This was our curriculum: *Sato Kagura* (regional Shinto shrine music) and *Matsuri Bayashi* (festival percussion), noh singing and dancing (*shimai*), kyogen, *shamisen* (*tokiwazu* style), Japanese classical dance, *rakugo* (comic storytelling), *gidayu* singing (narrative music for the puppet theater), *ningyo-zukai* (bunraku puppet handling), and *kiyari* (traditional work songs).

Of course, there was a kabuki component taught by Mitsugoro. This is the curriculum that Ishikawa and I formulated based on suggestions from Mitsugoro. All the teachers were top in their fields.

I hadn't really decided to become a kabuki actor; I just wanted to take lessons. This was out of curiosity more than anything else and at the time I was ready to try anything. Through the Saikagi Juku, I studied *rakugo* with Sanyutei Koencho. I went to him with a letter of introduction. Shincho and Encho, two professional *rakugo* storytellers who are now famous, were training with him at that time.

When Koencho taught *rakugo* he would tell the story once, then say, "Give it a try," and have the student tell it, copying his teacher as much as possible. If the student forgot a portion, Koencho would say, "It goes like this here, doesn't it?" The third time through the student would tell a ten- to fifteen-minute story by himself. This was how I found out that *rakugo* is learned in these one-on-one sessions with the teacher. First imitating his teacher as closely as possible and gradually learning to make it his own.

Later as part of the Toho Theater Troupe, I finally got to make use of this training when I performed *rakugo* as part of a production and even though I had forgotten most of the actual stories that I had learned, at least I had the confidence that comes from having studied with a master.

STUDYING WITH MATAGORO AFTER GRADUATION FROM COLLEGE

I graduated from Sophia University in 1957 and began serious training with the other members of the Saikagi Juku. It didn't even occur to me to look for a full-time job like all the other college graduates. Ishikawa was not about to let me go after all the training he'd given me, and anyway, the Saikagi Juku was no longer just me—there were now ten other students.

Eventually we had our first recital, and a few reporters happened to show up. When they said that they had found our methods of study intriguing, I was thrilled and felt that the value of what we were doing was confirmed. I couldn't leave the others now; as one of the first members I felt as though the school would fall apart if I didn't attend.

The school was on the other side of Tokyo from my home and I was taking the Yamanote loop line line to Tabata and walking to the rehearsal hall at Ogu almost every day. I would often end up spending the night there. Even so, I still hadn't definitely decided to become an actor.

I avoided my father at home because I felt as though I would be disowned any moment. I spent all morning furiously helping with his *konnyaku* business, and then would run off at noon. I wouldn't return until late at night. I wasn't the only one, though. The students in our group were nearly all people who had dropped out of school, or were studying for entrance exams, or already specializing in Japanese classical dance. None of us was leading a particularly normal or respectable life.

I met my teacher Matagoro around this time. Mitsugoro was teaching dance and directing Takechi Tetsuji's kabuki troupe in Kyoto in addition to teaching and performing in Tokyo, so he was constantly travelling between the two cities. We were about to begin learning *Kurumabiki* (The Carriage Fight), when Mitsugoro had to leave Tokyo for Kyoto. He introduced us to his younger brother with instructions that we were to study with him in Mitsugoro's absence.

My first impression was that it was strange that they were brothers since they didn't look at all alike. That was because Matagoro was the husband of Mitsugoro's younger sister and therefore a brother by marriage. Matagoro had a charm all his own and from that time he often asked me to help with odd jobs.

I was fortunate to meet Matagoro because of his wide knowledge of the kabuki theater. He was quite famous as a child actor, which was fortunate since his father had died while he was very young and so he had to support his family by himself, earning the salary of an adult actor. He received the protection and help of some of the greatest actors of the time and so, when I met him, he had many decades of seeing great performances at first hand. Moreover, his memory is prodigious and he knows many roles that he has never acted himself, simply from having been in the same production.

When we studied with Matagoro, instead of formal lessons we would go to see him from time to time and ask him to teach us something. He would select some kabuki speech and teach it to us, taking great care with the rhythm and intonation. This is the way that actors learn the techniques of kabuki declamation and the tones used for various role types. There are great classics and famous scenes in kabuki, but it is much more important to learn the fundamentals of kabuki—the role types and movement and speech appropriate to each type and to be able to perform a particular role type instantly at any time. Matagoro was also teaching young actors from famous kabuki families, so that sometimes we were able to have lessons together with them.

BECOMING A PROFESSIONAL KABUKI ACTOR

In 1961 there occurred an event that rocked the kabuki world. In May of that year, Matsumoto Koshiro VIII, one of the highest-ranking kabuki actors, and Nakamura Matagoro II, my teacher, led about thirty actors from the fold at Shochiku, which had nearly monopolized kabuki, to its archrival in the entertainment business, Toho. This shook Shochiku, which was increasingly emphasizing its large elegant theaters at the expense of a kabuki close to a popular audience. The prospect of a kabuki troupe to rival Shochiku's aroused visions of all sorts of new possibilities.

My teacher Mitsugoro said, "Matagoro is going to Toho—why don't you go with him? Don't let this opportunity slip by. This might be the only chance for an actor with as late a start as you to become a professional." I discussed the matter with Iizawa, and he thought that it might work out as long as I was going with Matagoro and had his support and protection.

Fortunately, I had another ally at Toho, a man named Chiya Michio, whom I knew through Iizawa Tadasu. Chiya had worked in the literature department at Shochiku and had written a prize-winning play for the great kabuki actor Nakamura Kichiemon I. When Koshiro and Matagoro moved to Toho, Chiya went with them and was in charge of the day-to-day details of production.

It was Chiya who formally introduced me to the Toho company, and in 1962, with his recommendation, I was cast in the Toho Theater Troupe's productions of *Butsuda to Songoku*, a modern version of the Chinese classic, "Monkey," and *Yoshitsune Senbon Zakura*, one of the great classics of kabuki. This was my first appearance on stage as a professional actor. I was not alone, either. Four other men from the Saikagi Juku were also cast. At least we had all made it to the point where our training allowed us to get paid for our work in theater.

The producers put us to work quickly since we had already studied *tachimawari* fight movements and dance. Moreover, since there were only thirty-six actors in the entire Toho Theater Troupe, they were short-handed and even actors like us could get roles, which means that we were unusually fortunate, even if they weren't starring roles.

In *Yoshitsune Senbon Zakura* there is a scene on the beach of Daimotsu which deals with a famous historical episode from the twelfth-century war between the Heike and Genji clans. The Heike clan had achieved great power and even placed an heir on the imperial throne. However, the rival Genji clan fought for control, eventually winning, and making its leader Yoritomo the first shogun. During the final sea battle, seeing that the situation was hopeless, lady-in-waiting Ni-no-Ama took the boy emperor Antoku in her arms and plunged into the ocean. In the kabuki version the emperor does not die but is handed over into the safekeeping of the Genji general Yoshitsune, and Ni-no-Ama commits suicide, giving her a dramatic death scene. In this scene I was cast as the soldier who holds the Emperor Antoku. Matagoro played Ni-no-Ama. The role of the boy emperor is one of those that is usually played by the heir of an important kabuki family.

There should have been no problem just holding the child playing the Emperor, but my hands suddenly felt very warm. Before I knew it, he had wet his pants. This pants-wetter has now grown into a fine kabuki actor. If he tries to act tough with me now, I put him in his place by saying, "Remember the scene at the coast of Daimotsu?"

There were no lines, I just had to hold the child Emperor in my arms. In kabuki these walk-on roles are called *shidashi*. This is the kind of role that normally goes to the actors in the *obeya*, the big communal dressing room on the third floor at a kabuki theater. I wanted to complain vigorously, but it turned out to be a good experience. I was not only getting paid but I got to appear on stage with giants like Matsumoto Koshiro and Ichikawa Chusha. Since the troupe was actually a bit too small for kabuki, there were always roles open for hard-working actors.

FIRST IMPORTANT ROLE AS A STAND-IN

Two years after joining Toho, in 1964, we were performing a new play at the Meiji-za. The plot was based on the classical kabuki theme of political turmoil in the great feudal house of Date. As usual, I entered the dressing room an hour before curtain. Chiya came running from the production department and said, "Please stand in for this role." While I was being told what to do I was put in costume, and before I knew it, I was on stage.

The star, Nakamura Mannosuke, who is now Nakamura Kichiemon II, had suffered an acute case of stomach cramps and had gone to the hospital. I had been appearing in a role without any lines, but since it had been about a week since we opened, I knew most of the lines of the play.

The actor playing the father, Ichikawa Chusha VIII was well known for being extremely exacting and for not hesitating to express himself if he was not pleased. And, just as expected, he complained about what I was doing. But he did it while we were on stage right in the middle of the performance.

The son says, "Father!" and draws close to his father, looking up at him with his eyes full of tears. His father then says, "I'm depending on you to take care of everything after I'm gone . . . ," and can't continue speaking, holding back his tears. After this, Chusha, as the father, has an extremely tense scene where he commits ritual suicide.

I said, "Father!" but Chusha didn't respond. I had no idea what to do, so I looked at him and he glared at me and mumbled, "You're too far downstage." I couldn't understand right away. Again he whispered, "You're out too far. Move back out of the way!"

His voice was too soft for the audience to hear but it sounded like thunder to me. It finally became clear that in sliding forward I had gone too far. In order to turn towards me, Chusha would have to turn away from the audience. I was mortified and had no choice but to slide back.

Instantly the response came, "I'm depending on you to take care of everything after I'm gone." Chusha's eyes were full of tears, he played the scene to the hilt, and, as though nothing had gone wrong, he calmly made his exit. Once again I was struck by the amazing self-possesion that a real kabuki star has.

I am proud of one particular part of my performance as a stand-in for this role, the part where the character had to sing a passage of noh music. Since Mitsugoro had said that a kabuki actor must know the noh theater, I had studied noh singing during my Saikagi Juku days. As a result I could take perform this scene without a hitch.

I was proud to learn from this experience that I had not been mistaken in my training. My start as a kabuki actor may have been extremely late, but I was happy to learn that the things I had learned with the Saikagi Juku were not going to go to waste.

Eventually, for a variety of reasons, Toho kabuki came to an end. Koshiro and his sons returned to Shochiku and Toho stopped putting on kabuki productions. But some of the actors stayed with Toho, performing modern theater and making special appearances with Shochiku kabuki from time to time. These included my teacher Matagoro, and when he appears at the Kabuki-za I usually go with him to assist him on and off stage, and to appear in a minor role. Unlike the actors at Shochiku, who rarely appear on stage outside of kabuki productions, a mixed repertoire of kabuki and modern theater is part of our regular performance schedule.

In 1966, with the establishment of the National Theater, new opportunities opened up. Nakamura Matagoro became head of a training program for young actors, and I have been fortunate enough to help him in preparing future kabuki actors. One reason that I have been able to do this lies in the fact that I have been formally recognized as a kabuki actor by reaching the rank of *nadai*.

ACHIEVING THE RANK OF *NADAI*

I achieved the rank of *nadai* in 1967. My decision to apply for it was formed the previous December, while I was appearing in

the classic kabuki play, *Sugawara Denju Tenarai Kagami*
(Sugawara and the Secrets of Calligraphy) at the National
Theater, and the important actor Nakamura Shikaku recommended that I try to become a *nadai*. But there were some difficulties to overcome.

One prerequisite for the *nadai* rank is to have had over ten
years of experience as the *deshi* or disciple of an actor. Since I
did not appear on stage until 1962, there seemed to be no way to
fulfil this condition.

Mitsugoro saved me by saying that we could count my time in
kabuki from the time I started studying with him instead of
from my first appearance on a kabuki stage. He said, " I'll make
sure everyone knows that this is the way we're going to count
your years of experience."

There are three ranks of *nadai*: *onadai*, *chunadai* and
hiranadai (major *nadai*, middle *nadai*, and ordinary *nadai*). Major
kabuki roles are played by *onadai*, while the supporting roles are
played by *chunadai*. The kind of roles an actor plays is determined by the status of his family. The actors who play the main
roles, the *onadai*, are the bosses of the kabuki theater world;
among others these include the families that originally held the
right to put on plays in the Edo period, the Morita Kanya,
Nakamura Kanzaburo, and Ichimura Uzaemon families. The
chunadai are below them in rank, and then the *hiranadai*.
Although there is no formal way of separating these ranks, this is
the way that actors think about the status of kabuki actors.

As a rule, the privileged sons of *onadai* must also take the test
to become *nadai*. Even Nakamura Utaemon, the present head
of the Haiyu Kyokai (Kabuki Performers' Association) and the
most influential actor in the kabuki world, had his sons take the
test before they became *nadai*. In fact, Utaemon's son Fukusuke
took the test at the same time that I did.

But there are also sons of famous actors who do not take the
test. This is because, as the sons of famous families, some have
played important roles from the time that they are small
children and even without a test their ability is apparent. This is
taken for granted, but it can nevertheless arouse indignation
amongst actors in the *obeya*.

There is a written test and a performance test for *nadai*. Of course the performance part is the crucial test, but still, out of a hundred points on the written test, I scored eighty-five. By contrast, the son of an *onadai* scored only fifteen points. This was a victory indeed.

Mitsugoro helped me. He had given me a dozen or so books on kabuki and suggested that I read them for future reference. If there was anything I was used to, it was studying for exams, so before the test I organized the materials and memorized them. I had a sense of what kind of questions might appear on the test. First of all, Mitsugoro was making up the questions. My intuition told me that the kinds of things he was always talking about would probably appear and I took care to study those points. And I was right. If I had studied a bit more carefully, I might even have achieved a perfect score.

These were the questions on my test:

1) What kind of footwear was worn by samurai in the Edo period when they went to their master's castle on public business?

2) In the play *Ise Ondo*, what is the name of the character that comes running in on the *hanamichi*, what is he searching for and what is the name of that object?

3) Is it proper form to mount a horse from the left side or the right side?

4) What are the origins of the phrases *shinogi o kezuru* (lit. "to carve a ridge on a sword," meaning "to fight vigorously"), and *seppa tsumaru* (lit. "pressed to a part of the hilt of a sword," meaning "to be at a loss")? Explain the origins by drawing a diagram.

5) When a *koshimoto* (lady-in-waiting) is on duty, is it proper for her to hold a lantern in her right hand or her left hand?

These questions, and their answers, give some idea of the kind of information considered important in the kabuki world. Here are the answers:

1) When a samurai goes to his master's castle, he wears straw sandals called *fuku zori*. These sandals are several layers thick and since most commoners wore sandals only a single layer thick, they indicated the wealth and rank of samurai as well as the for-

mality of the occasion. Here, and in the last three questions, we can see the need for kabuki actors to be familiar with the details of samurai life.

2) The play *Ise Ondo Koi no Netaba* is about a former samurai named Mitsugi who serves at the great Ise shrine. He is attempting to help the family of his former master by finding a treasured sword named *Aoi Shimozaka*. He has found the sword, but when he visits his favorite teahouse, the sword is put into a different sheath. The answer to the question is Mitsugi, a sword, and *Aoi Shimozaka*. Ironically, he is carrying the sword himself, not knowing it because the sheath is different. There is also a curse on the sword and once drawn it will not rest until it has killed, and when Mitsugi draws this sword, this leads to the multiple killing that is the climax of this play. This question shows the need to be intimately familiar with the standard repertoire of kabuki.

3) In the West horses are mounted from the left side, but in old Japan it was exactly opposite and Japanese saddles are made to be mounted from the right.

4) Both phrases are common in Japanese, and refer to parts of a sword. *Shinogi* is a kind of ridge on the sword, and when two swordmen are fighting it is this part of the sword that engages the other so that the phrase means to fight vigorously. *Seppa* is the end of the hilt of a sword, the part farthest away from the cutting tip. So to be pushed to the very hilt of the sword means to be in a very desperate situation.

5) A lady-in-waiting or a samurai always holds a lantern in the left hand, leaving the right hand free to carry a weapon, a sword in the case of a samurai and a halberd in the case of a lady-in-waiting.

Nadai is a short version of the term *nadai yakusha* or *nadai* actor, and means a major kabuki actor. This is how the *Kabuki Dictionary*, edited by Yamamoto Jiro, describes it:

> The sons of important actors advance quickly; others find it much more difficult to get the opportunities that will allow them to advance to the status of *nadai*. For this reason, beginning late in the Taisho period (1912–1926), a system was set up to choose candidates and to give *nadai* status after testing

their knowledge and performing skills. After becoming a *nadai,* the actor no longer has to be in the *obeya,* the collective dressing room on the third floor or the collective dressing rooms for *onnagata* on the second floor, but receive individual dressing rooms and are allowed to have personal attendants. In addition, their remuneration increases and their names appear on the official program (*banzuke*).

This is the theory, but in reality things are a bit different. This is especially true with respect to dressing rooms. Today *nadai* dressing rooms, whether for *onnagata* or actors of male roles, hold five or six actors.

Nevertheless, within kabuki there is a world of difference between being and not being *nadai.* It makes an actor happy to see his name on the special marquee that they put up for events like *kaomise* productions, called an *iori kanban,* meaning a special signboard with a roof over it. The sight of your name there written in the special script used for kabuki really makes you feel like a kabuki actor. This tradition should never change.

Having passed the *nadai* test is not just the lowest common denominator among kabuki actors. Without this qualification, even if an actor has been working for forty or fifty years, he remains in the *obeya* until he passes the test. That there are many such actors is a special characteristic of the kabuki world.

Many of the *obeya* actors cannot play the *shamisen* or dance, but not because they are lazy or not interested in polishing their artistic skills. They cannot improve because they are kept so busy assisting their masters that they have no time to go to lessons or practice on their own. In fact, there are still actors who treat their *deshi* as errand boys and menial servants. On this point my own teacher Nakamura Matagoro is probably critical as well.

One reason that so many prospective kabuki actors go through the training program at the National Theater instead of going directly to actors to be accepted as *deshi* is because they have come to dislike such a system. If one goes to an actor directly to become a *deshi,* one is likely to end up doing errands or menial jobs. Art is the sort of thing that cannot be improved unless one works at it every waking hour even at the expense of sleep. The *deshi* simply don't get time to do this. Out of six plays performed in the matinee and evening programs, there are some actors who have their *deshi* appear in one play and then assist for three or four other plays. This system benefits only the actors, because the *deshi*'s pay comes from the production company and not out of the actor's pocket.

The result of this misguided system that somehow became established in kabuki is that there are now actors who cannot play the *shamisen* and actors who cannot dance. This has contributed to the lowering of the quality of kabuki. Even if actors are able to eat regularly, if, in the process the quality of the art itself is lowered, isn't the result meaningless?

To continue, the performance test was held the day after the written test in the small hall of the National Theater. Candidates were to take parts in actual plays, and roles were decided by lottery. The program for my test was a historical play called *Kagamiyama Kokyo-no-Nishiki-e* and a dance called *Noriaibune Eho Manzai*. We had two weeks before the performance to learn and master the roles. The short rehearsal time tested our knowledge of the fundamentals of kabuki. I drew the role of *tayu* or leading entertainer.

It was the starring role in *Noriaibune*, which depicts a group of people on a ferry-boat, and it has the most to dance, but fortunately I had been studying *tokiwazu*, the style of music that accompanies this dance, since my college days. I was lucky to draw it because I already knew the piece. Moreover, on the day of the performance my teacher Tokiwazu Mojisuke played the *shamisen* so that I danced to the accompaniment of someone I was already used to.

I scored seventy out of a hundred points and passed. The result was that eight of the ten examiners recommended me for *nadai*. Out of eight people taking the test, four passed. The examiners that did not recommend me were two kabuki actors from the Kansai region, who had no idea who I was. This was natural since I had only been on stage for five years and had never had the chance to act together with these *onadai* from the Kansai.

It was a bit out of order, but I had formally become a *deshi* of Matagoro in 1964, which was before taking the *nadai* test. I had entered Toho with him, but hesitated to formally become a *deshi* because I had seen all too many examples of *deshi* who were used as menial servants and thus had no chance to improve their acting.

My interest in becoming a *deshi* was also dulled by the advice I was given. Ishikawa was totally against my becoming a kabuki actor. Chiya Michio, despite the fact that he was the producer, said, "You got such a late start as an actor that it's better not to try." He said that I should continue to act under my own family name of Ito instead of formally becoming a kabuki actor and taking my teacher's artistic family name. I had reached the stage when I had to make my own decisions, and knew that I could not delay making a decision indefinitely. Finally I decided to formally become Matagoro's *deshi*. I was an uninvited *deshi*, but Matagoro said, "Go right ahead," and accepted me immediately. It must have been difficult for Matagoro to teach someone who had been a student of his older brother.

Matagoro yells at his other three *deshi* all the time, but he never used to yell at me. Recently, though, he has started to correct me more frequently, and this makes me quite happy, because I think it means that have finally become something of an insider. Looking back on it now, I must have been a rather difficult *deshi* for Matagoro to handle. This may be true even now.

The "Middle-Aged" Kabuki Actor

I became a kabuki actor only through the combination of many lucky circumstances. I was first able to appear in Toho kabuki as an actor because Matagoro and the other actors joined Toho. If there had never been Toho kabuki, and if all that time Shochiku had continued to monopolize kabuki, as far I know I might have been a television director by now.

If there had not been Toho kabuki, I probably would not have become a kabuki actor. I was twenty-three when I graduated from college and twenty-five when I first appeared with the Toho Theater Troupe. This is terribly old for a beginning actor. There are other examples of actors joining kabuki that late, but kabuki is the sort of world where it is almost unimaginable for such an actor to reach the status of *nadai*.

I don't think that I would have been able to stand up to ten years of hard work as an *obeya* actor. The actors from the Saikagi Juku who went to Toho with me almost all quit after that one experience. They thought that the kabuki world was extremely feudal, and that its hierarchy was too sharp and inflexible. For people accustomed to the normal world, the kabuki theater can be a hard place to work.

I know the normal world as well as the theater world, and maybe because of that, somewhere in me there is something detached from the theater. All my life I've never really felt I was totally an actor. Before I became an actor, I paid to see theater and now get paid both to watch and to act. What could be better? In other words, I do this because I like it. In this respect there will always be something of the amateur in me.

CHAPTER 4

A Tour of the *Gakuya* (Backstage)

Behind the world of the kabuki stage is the social world of the backstage area, which nourishes and breathes life into every performance. For practical reasons, many things are modern backstage, and for equally practical reasons, many things are very traditional, so much so in fact that at times it seems like things have not changed much since the Edo period. Let's take a quick look backstage at the Kabuki-za. In Japanese, the entire area is known as the *gakuya*, which literally means "dressing room." The star dressing rooms are the heart of the backstage area.

Around the corner from the front entrance of the massive Japanese-style ferro-concrete Kabuki-za is the entrance to the *gakuya*. The actual door is set back from the sidewalk several yards, and to the right of the walk to the door is a driveway that leads to the garage, which has a very few, highly coveted, parking spaces for the stars' cars—that is, for those who are important enough to rate a parking space but don't come by chauffeured limousine. Most of the actors come to the theater by train and subway.

The entire driveway is set back into the Kabuki-za office building and protected from the elements. Out here there is usually a jumble of odd items. Space is at a premium at the Kabuki-za, so much so that some things are stored out here, perhaps a luxurious palanquin that belongs to props, or the packing cases for actors' personal belongings. There might also be a few pots with the withered remains of the plants and flowers

71

that are among the presents showered on the stars of kabuki by their fans.

Through the old glass door to the *gakuya* one can peek straight through, along a corridor lined with dressing rooms, to a dressing room at the end with a *noren* split curtain discreetly guarding it from outsider's eyes. The bold three rice-measure pattern is the family crest of the most prestigious name in kabuki, Ichikawa Danjuro. Before pushing open the glass door, if you take a detour and go around the side of the *gakuya* building, you can see the sandpit used by low-ranking actors for practicing the flips and somersaults that are the foundation of fight scenes (*tachimawari*) in kabuki.

STAGE DOOR

Once you swing open the door of the *gakuya* you are in the entrance area, which is a step lower than the main *gakuya*. Just inside the front door of Japanese houses there is always an entrance hall for removing the shoes. Inside one wears slippers, except when entering individual rooms with *tatami* mats on the floor. Kabuki theaters follow the same custom.

On each side of the entrance hall there are shelves filled by pairs of shoes neatly arranged and labeled with the names of their owners. The entrance to the *gakuya* is watched over by an old man called the *kuchiban*. He offers stars their personal *zori* slippers and takes their street shoes, placing them in the appropriately labeled cabinet. Less important actors and staff take care of their own footwear, exchanging their street shoes for the slippers which sit on the open shelves closer to the door.

The entrance is set lower than the main hallway, to mark the boundary between inside and outside. Each room backstage is also constructed this way, so that the slippers that actors put on when entering the backstage area are shed before entering anyone's room. Even onstage space is defined by actors taking off and putting on their shoes and, in a dance, this ritual denotes different sections. When an actor takes off his shoes it means that the character is inside and his actions assume a more intimate atmosphere.

The old man by the glass door asks visitors their business and greets everyone with the ubiquitous *Ohayo gozaimasu* (good morning), which is used in the theater and throughout the Japanese entertainment world as the first greeting of the day or night regardless of the time. If an actor is very important or perhaps elderly, he may be met at the door by some of his *deshi*, a word that means student or disciple and in kabuki means a low-ranking actor in an actor's service. The kabuki world, especially backstage, is governed by a precise and complex sense of hierarchy and mutual deference and obligation. From the moment we enter the *gakuya* we can feel the strong sense of clan and hierarchy that pervades the place.

Once we step up into the main part of the *gakuya* we enter a hallway that runs straight back to the current Ichikawa Danjuro's dressing room. The most important dressing rooms are on this floor. To the right of Danjuro's dressing room is the entrance to the stage. To the left there is a sink and some bathrooms, and the hallway bends and then continues straight on. Closer to us, on the left, is the costume room. In front of us to our right is another old man keeping watch over a board studded with red pegs.

The man sits behind a counter and keeps track of which actors have arrived by checking the *chakutoban*, a board where the actors insert wooden pegs next to their names handwritten in the florid calligraphy of kabuki. He is called the *todori* and, although he may seem just a minor functionary he, like many other peripheral people in this world, is a valuable resource. He has seen decades of kabuki. He can tell an actor that his father or even his grandfather performed a particular role in a particular way, he can remember costuming, scene and line changes. The actor uses this knowledge along with his own experience to guide what traditions he will use in his performance. The *todori* does not have to be old, but he is responsible for very delicate matters like allocating dressing rooms, and years of experience are very useful in dealing with a world so sensitive to rank and prerogative.

Directly above the *todori*'s window is a small shrine adorned with the strips of paper that set off a Shinto shrine, and with offerings of bottles of *sake* rice wine. Each bottle has the name of the actor that offered it, usually one of the more important actors who feel responsible for the success of this month's production. As the actors check in, many of them will pause for a moment, clap, and stand in an attitude of prayer to show their respect for the shrine. Theater is such a chancy business that its members will call on all kinds of help to ensure the success of a production. The shrine is designed to appeal to all gods and all sects. The Kabuki Performers' Association headed by Nakamura Utaemon, and to which over 200 kabuki actors belong, does not restrict the practicing of any religion, but forbids active membership of any political party.

The *todori* faces a color television monitor on the wall of the hallway showing the action on stage. This is the only television monitor backstage; in their own dressing rooms, the actors must make do with antique speakers that give only the sounds on stage. Like actors in western theaters, kabuki actors keep track of their cues by listening to these squawk boxes.

There is, however, also a more traditional way of getting cues. The famous clappers or *hyoshigi* mark the end of a play with a stream of claps that increases gradually in frequency and intensity as the curtain is drawn shut. The clappers can also signal a variety of other things. Two short claps between scenes means "to be continued," in other words, no intermission. A clap backstage is the equivalent of a five-minute call. Operating these clappers is one of the responsibilities of the *kyogen sakusha*, who are in charge of coordinating a play like stage managers.

The room where the *todori* sits is called the *sakusha beya* or "playwright's room." Behind him you might see some men dressed in black. These men are the *kyogen sakusha* or playwrights. In the Edo period they actually wrote the plays, but today they are more like a combination of assistant director and stage manager, responsible for scripts, and general coordination of a play. When a play is so traditional that a new script is not printed, they are also responsible for writing out each actor's lines. The men in this post come from a family line established by Kawatake Mokuami, the last great Edo playwright. They take the name Takeshiba as their professional family name.

COSTUMERS

In the hallway beyond the counter, there are boxes on their

sides forming shelves lining the sides of the walls. These are filled with neatly folded costumes. Lavish silk kimono for courtesans and geisha, padded costumes in bright colors for the samurai in period plays, and more sober, ordinary kimono for the characters in domestic plays can be seen peeking out of the boxes. A look inside the door on the left reveals the cramped costumer's room. There is a shelf up to the ceiling along the right wall. But even so, space is at a premium and costumes have to kept in the hallway as well. This room is constantly busy with costumers taking costumes to stars' dressing rooms, returning later to dress them, and bringing back piles of costumes that have been worn, taking out any stains with benzine, ironing them and then folding them for the following day's performance. Costumers also have to go into the wings of the stage area to dress stars if the costumes are too unwieldy to be piloted through the backstage area. They sometimes take the stars' costumes off in the wings to minimize wear and tear on immensely expensive costumes. The minor actors usually have to fend for themselves, changing on the third floor without the aid of *deshi* and costumers.

One of the most spectacular costume change techniques is called *hikinuki*. Usually, in a dance play, the dancer will pause briefly, facing the audience, as his stage assistants unobtrusively pull out cords holding his costume together. Then the dancer stands still, and the assistants pull on the kimono, which breaks away to reveal an entirely different color and pattern underneath. The stage assistants tug on little balls which are attached to stout cords holding the upper layer of kimono onto the lower. The cords are attached at the top and bottom of the kimono sleeves and on the bottom hem and the balls are covered with material the same color as the kimono to make them unobtrusive.

If the costume comes apart each day, it has to be sewn up again as well, and the costume room is where that takes place. The costumer in charge of a particular actor's costumes sews the separate pieces together with light basting thread and then threads through the heavy cords that will be pulled out on stage. While one costumer does this, the others continue with the usual activities of the costume room when it is quiet, namely, ironing, eating, watching television, and playing cards.

The Stage

We are now directly in front of Danjuro's dressing room and need to step back. A play has just ended and all the actors are leaving the stage, stars first with black-clad *deshi* in their wake and the minor actors afterward, always maintaining the order of the hierarchy. Before going on through the *gakuya* we might take a peek at the stage. A turn to the right and we are facing a large mirror where an actor can check his appearance before his entrance. Now left and after going up a short ramp we are walking along the back wall of the stage.

Here on the stage it is even more important to have changed to slippers at the door. One absolutely firm rule is that one never walks on a kabuki stage wearing shoes unless one is playing a role that requires them. The stage at the Kabuki-za is enormous, and even when there is a play going on, there is room on the back half of the revolving stage for another whole set.

Every time a scene change is made, whether the curtain is open or not, the revolving stage is used. While one scene is being played on the front part of the stage, another scene can be put up or removed on the back part of the stage. The larger flat pieces are set in place and then platforms, walls and doors are added. If one looks up at the fly loft, one can see that most of the flats have their bare undecorated sides toward the audience. This is because the set is put together on the back half of the revolving stage facing the rear of the stage, and, once complete, the set will soon be brought into the audience's sight by the revolving stage.

All around us the stage crew is busy putting up the set. Some, especially if they will be seen on stage at some point, are in traditional dress, with black *tabi* divided socks, heavy short-sleeved jacket and close fitting leggings. Others are wearing jeans and sweatshirts.

On Stage

On the Western stage, the part of the stage farthest from the audience is called "upstage" and the part closest to the audience is called "downstage." This is partly because the stage was once sloped so that action on the back of the stage could be seen, and the back of the stage was actually higher than the front. This was never the case on the kabuki stage. The side of the stage to the audience's right is called the *kamite* or upstage, the side of the stage to the audience's left is called the *shimote* or downstage.

In production this is usually used to indicate status. Higher ranking characters are usually closer to the *kamite*, lower ranking characters are placed on the *shimote* side. Other considerations of general visual composition also come into play, of course, but this is, fundamentally, the way that characters are placed on stage. When new characters appear, changing the relative status of the characters already on stage, all the actors stand and reassemble in accordance with the new patterns of status and deference.

BACKGROUND MUSIC: THE GEZA

On the audience's left is a black grille, which conceals a room containing the background musicians. Perhaps because of its position on the "lower" side of the stage, the place of the background musicians is called the *geza* or "lower seat." From backstage the black screen is revealed as just a partition. Behind it is a waist-high platform on which the *shamisen* players, who provide the bulk of the background music sit, formal kneeling style, looking out through a screen at the action on stage and the audience. Behind them is a table with a variety of percussion instruments; beside it is the most important instrument, the *odaiko* or large drum. This drum is sounded in a variety of patterns to indicate the beginning or ending of a program or to evoke natural phenomena like wind, rain, and even snow.

Often dialogue on stage will be accompanied by quiet *shamisen* music in the background. When scenes open and when new characters make their entrances there are snatches of song that set the mood on stage. The singers usually move in and out of the *geza*, only staying long enough to sing their particular portions.

PROPS

Past the *geza* in the "downstage" direction, there is a storage space with the props for the current production. There are always immense quantities of props required for each production because so many kabuki plays turn on subtle points of class and customs. A simple pipe can be a geisha's pipe with a long red stem and small bowl at the end, or a high-ranking courtesan's pipe in the same shape but larger and made of silver. It also might be an immense pipe with a fat, heavily decorated stem, the kind of pipe used by larger-than-life villains in period pieces. An audience member familiar with kabuki would understand volumes about a particular character just by looking at the details of the props that he uses. This means that the job of the propman is difficult indeed, and he has large boxes full of the props to be used in the following scene and the props that he has just gathered up from the last scene.

THE UNDERWORLD: NARAKU

While the scene shifters continue their work, let's go back to the entrance to the stage. There is also a staircase going down below the stage. Down here there are a few odd dressing rooms, but the space is mostly devoted to storage and stage machinery. Here we can see the motors that turn the revolving stage and that operate the various lifts in the stage floor. Sometimes if a play involves very fast changes a slide may be used to allow an actor to drop below the stage through a trapdoor so that he can run to the other end of the *hanamichi* for a shockingly quick entrance. If we walk on past the machinery, we will see a passageway that runs under the *hanamichi*. This entire basement is known as the *naraku* which means, appropriately enough, "hell".

A look at the beginning of the passageway under the *hanamichi* reveals a lift called a *suppon* that is used to raise actors onto the *hanamichi*. This particular lift is only used on special occasions, especially to reveal ghosts and other supernatural creatures. At the far end of this passage are some more stairs that go to the room at the end of the *hanamichi*. There is also a large mirror here and an actor can make final adjustments or even have his costume put on here before the *agemaku* curtain concealing him is opened with a sharp clatter of its curtain rings and he makes his entrance.

Now if we leave the stage, go back the way we came, then go all the way to the end of the hallway to the right, we come to the stairs that lead to the upper levels of the *gakuya*.

There are basically three floors to the *gakuya*. The first two floors have star dressing rooms and the third floor has somewhat larger collective dressing rooms for two or three *nadai* actors at a time, divided into ones for the actors of male roles and ones for the actors of female roles, and then there is the *obeya*, the large mass dressing room for actors below the rank of *nadai*.

BACKSTAGE AT THE NATIONAL THEATER

The *gakuya* at the National Theater, which was built in 1966 next to the moat that encircles the Imperial Palace, is laid out differently. The backstage area is at the back of the main building, which contains two halls: the large hall (1,600 seats), and the small hall (630 seats). There are two doors into the backstage area, one for staff members and visitors and another for actors. Inside there is a shrine facing the entrance, in front of the *chakutoban* and the *sakusha beya*, but one feature of the *gakuya* area of the National Theater immediately strikes you— all the dressing rooms are on one floor. There is another floor above, but it is used for offices. Although there are dressing rooms of different sizes ranged down either side of wide corridor, there is no long-standing tradition of certain dressing rooms belonging to specific actors.

There is also a smaller building, often decorated with colorful banners, at the back of the main complex. It houses both a 600-seat hall for *rakugo* (Japanese comic story-telling) and the studios of the National Theater Training Program.

A STAR DRESSING ROOM

At the Kabuki-za, a real star gets a suite with two rooms on the first floor. The outer door is marked with a *noren*, which is a split curtain, usually, in the case of a top actor, made of silk. The *noren* has the crest of the actor or perhaps some other design associated with a particular actor or his acting family, which will be inscribed, "From his fan club," or something similar. Once inside the dressing room proper, there is a little space for taking off one's shoes and a step up into the outer room. Often there

A star's dressing room at the National Theater, Tokyo. Well-wishers and lesser actors pay their respects and make their greetings in the outer room.

will be a rack for swords in this entrance hall. In some ways this is a remnant of the days when samurai would visit actors and deposit their swords on the rack before entering the dressing room. But it isn't just tradition that keeps the rack there. More concretely, this rack is used for the swords and other props that an actor uses on stage.

The outer room is a kind of waiting room and storage area. The fortunate stars have sinks in these outer rooms, big broad sinks that they can use to wash off their makeup. They are usually very old-fashioned sinks set at floor level so that they can be used from a kneeling position. The outer room also serves as a kind of waiting room for visitors while the actor is occupied with other business in the inner room. Moreover, the sliding door between the outer and inner dressing rooms is a very important symbolic boundary. Each day all the other actors in the company come to pay greetings to the star actor. Unless invited in, or unless they have special business, the actors just kneel, open the sliding door, bow and say *ohayo gozaimasu*.

An actor's mirror is the heart of his dressing room. These are usually large adjustable mirrors set on top of a low chest of drawers. They are usually made of the finest wood, with luxurious inlay or carvings, and are usually presented by an actor's patrons or fan club on the occasion of taking a distinguished acting name. Of course, these are meant to be used from a kneeling position as well, and the actor will usually kneel on a thick cushion, and spread a cloth over his lap as he puts on his makeup.

Everything in the dressing room is set up to make the actor feel at home. Around him will be floral tributes from admirers, both cut flowers and potted plants—the plants should last for at least twenty-five days, the usual length of a run. The top dressing rooms have a decorative alcove or *tokonoma* and the actor will hang a scroll there and perhaps display some piece of porcelain as well. There will often be a low coffee table and some chairs in the room, for this is where an actor receives visitors and conducts his business.

The sense of tradition is overwhelming in the dressing room. At the Kabuki-za, an actor may occupy a dressing room that has been used by previous holders of his name for almost the last century. The most prestigious actors, that is, those coming from established kabuki acting lines, always get the same dressing rooms. Less exalted actors may have to change their dressing rooms from month to month depending on the exact production and their relative status within it. The scroll in the alcove may be a picture that is related to a role that the actor is playing, or perhaps some calligraphy by an admired literary figure or famous actor. It also may be a scroll featuring an *oshiguma*—a piece of cloth which has been pressed onto an actor's face after he has played a role with *kumadori* make-up. Not only are the lines of the make-up transferred to the cloth, but because it is taken after a performance, it is a unique record of one day's interpretation of the role. Each *oshiguma* is special and an actor may hang one up as a clue to the art of his predecessor or as inspiration for his performance. There may be snapshots of famous actors of the past stuck onto an actor's mirror as well to remind him of what he has to live up to, and to make him meditate on how to match his models.

The star dressing room is the hub of the star actor's life and of all the people associated with him. A star usually has one non-actor to maintain the room, keep it clean, bring tea for visitors, and similar tasks. One or more of an actor's *deshi* will be on call to prepare his makeup, help apply it and to help him put on his costume. From time to time, an actor's manager might also visit.

An actor's individual personality and the characteristics of his particular acting tradition are important in the dressing room. Because he personally selects all the people working there and because all the *deshi* work to imitate their master in every way, each dressing room strongly reflects its occupant and has a unique atmosphere. For example, in general the dressing rooms of actors who specialize in male roles have a very different atmosphere from the dressing rooms of pure *onnagata*, who only play female roles. In the Edo period, *onnagata* were supposed to live as women off stage as well as on. Although today this is no longer true there is still something different about the dressing rooms of actors who specialize in feminine beauty.

A performance at the Kabuki-za generally goes from eleven in the morning to nine at night. If an actor is in the first and last play of a day's program, nearly every waking hour of his day revolves around the theater. The National Theater generally has one performance a day instead of two, and that performance usually lasts no more than three hours. Kabuki actors enjoy the modernity and convenience of the facilities at the National Theater, still, since it reflects so little of the hierarchy and tradition that govern the kabuki world, most actors think of their dressing rooms at the National Theater like hotel rooms, while their dressing rooms at Kabuki-za are like apartments in a building where everyone knows each other intimately and is always watching what everyone else is doing.

But, permanent as the dressing rooms at Kabuki-za may feel, at the end of each twenty-five day run all the actor's belongings must be packed up and moved. Even if the actor is appearing the next month, he will probably be in a different dressing room if he is not one of the top three or four actors in the kabuki world. Besides, often the theater is rented out for a dance recital or some other performance during the few days between runs of kabuki, and other people will use the dressing rooms during this time. The task of packing and unpacking an actor's belongings falls to his *deshi*, yet another job to keep the *deshi* busy off stage.

The most important dressing rooms are on the first floor, right next to the stairs to the second floor. Less prestigious actors get smaller and more inconvenient dressing rooms on the second floor. But the first and second floors are only for the *kanbu* actors, that is, star actors from important lineages. These actors are also called *onadai* or major *nadai*. All the minor actors, that is *hiranadai* and *nadai-shita* actors are on the third floor.

By the foot of the stairs is an inconspicuous glass-paneled door that leads to a barber shop. Now it provides a great convenience because actors can have their hair cut without leaving the theater but in the Edo period hairdressing was more important. Today men no longer shave the pate of their heads, but in the past, not only did most men shave the top of their heads—a kind of leftover from the military period when warriors did that to be more comfortable under hot and weighty helmets—but many of the hair styles on the kabuki stage were identical to current hair fashions outside the theater. Merchants in plays showing contemporary life looked much like merchants in the outside world. But for more exaggerated hair styles, especially in stylized period pieces, actors wore wigs. Before wigs could be put on their heads, their hair had to be redressed in a flat style that made room for a wig. After a day's performance was over, the actor could have his hair dressed again with the voluminous side locks and the rounded line of the loosely gathered hair in back that marked a well-groomed man. The barber shop is a reminder of an age when kabuki actors began and ended their days by having their hair done.

SECOND FLOOR: *TOKOYAMA*

If we go up the stairs to the second floor we will find more star dressing rooms. These dressing rooms are also quite prestigious, and the ones closest to the stairs are the most desirable. There is another shrine here, dedicated to Inari—the fox-spirit. In the Edo period the second floor or *chu-nikai* (lit. mezzanine) was reserved for *onnagata*, but this is no longer so. However, there is a reminder of this custom in the tiny little room here for the *toko-*

yama, who are in charge of the wigs for female roles.

There are cabinets all around this little space with the wigs for female roles. These can range from the simple and restrained wigs used by actors in the roles of humble wives in domestic plays to the elaborate and weighty wigs used by actors playing high-ranking courtesans. These wigs are covered with combs, glittering tiaras and other ornaments.

The *tokoyama* do not make the wigs, but they are responsible for putting them on the actors and making sure that the wigs look good. This can mean just patting it back into shape and combing a few stray strands of hair, or it can mean undoing the hairstyle and redoing it again, which is a very involved precedure. There is always a hot plate in the *tokoyama*'s room because he uses it to heat a special iron, a piece of metal that looks like a shoe tree, to straighten out hair when he redresses a wig. He also uses the iron to flatten out the straps of the *habutae,* that is, the cap that an actor puts on under the wig.

Usually the stars of kabuki are served by particular wig dressers since each actor has individual tastes in hair styles and particular preferences about the exact shape and balance of the wigs. Wig dressers also specialize in either male or female wigs and almost never have experience with both.

THIRD FLOOR

It's time to go to the third floor. Suddenly the stairs are much steeper than they are between the first and second floor, a sure sign that the people upstairs are lower in rank. If you turn right at the top of the stairs there are some medium-sized dressing rooms. Some of them are used by the musicians. Each variety of music gets its own dressing room, *nagauta, gidayu, tokiwazu* and the like. Sometimes they have dressing rooms on the first or second floor, but more often they are relegated to the third floor. Even though there may be elderly musicians among them, who are designated Living National Treasures by the Japanese government, within the theater the rank of musician is clearly below that of actor.

The medium-sized dressing rooms are used by *nadai* actors with some degree of seniority, such as myself, and must be shared with two or three actors to a room. A star dressing room may have decorations and elegant furniture, but one of these *nadai* dressing rooms is much more functional, with mirrored desks and hooks for the actors to hang up their clothes.

At the end of the hall is a largish room for the *tokoyama* in charge of male wigs. It is much larger than the room for the female wigs, but all the same, the walls are lined with shelves holding the stars' wigs.

At the top of the stairs, if you turn left instead of right you will be faced with a long stainless steel sink. You might see an actor standing here washing off his makeup. Walk around the sink and you are in a big room with low desks lining the wall all around. This is the *obeya* for all the lower ranking actors. Each desk is covered with a particular actor's makeup kit and mirrors. There is a strict order to the desks—an actor's position is judged by seniority based on when they entered the kabuki world.

There are usually around thirty actors in the *obeya*, but the number changes with the demands of each month's production. Some decades ago there were as many as a hundred actors in the *obeya* at a time, and their makeup desks not only lined the walls, but formed a double row down the center of the room. In winter there was only one heater (using charcoal for fuel) for the wide space, and the degree of proximity was determined by seniority . Nowadays, with central heating and the decline in number of actors, that particular hardship no longer exists. Now there are not enough actors to make a hundred at a time and the actors in the *obeya* tend to be extremely busy. As *deshi*, they generally try to arrive before their master to see that everything is ready for him. They dress in black and help in the dressing room and the wings while their master is on stage, and then have to rush to change and make up for their own appearances on stage. If work is light and a *deshi* and his master only have brief appearances on stage, a low-ranking actor may only have to be in the theater for a few hours. But at other times such an actor might have tiny roles in the first and last play on the day's programs, in which case he will have to be in the theater from ten in the morning to ten at night.

From top to bottom, the *gakuya* of a kabuki theater is not only a functional space, but reflects the intricate hierarchy of the kabuki world. Even though the interior is more or less modern, every day kabuki actors live and work in spaces that housed the great actors of the past and work alongside people that remember actors that may have died many decades ago. This is where they not only live with the recent past, but recreate the Edo period, both onstage and backstage.

CHAPTER 5

The Kabuki Way of Life

A kabuki actor's morning begins with lessons. An actor usually has to get to the *gakuya* by about 10:30, and before that he has a morning *shamisen* or dance lesson. Even though it's a lesson, in the case of kabuki actors these lessons are very simple things, just running through a short section of a piece four or five times, then formally thanking the teacher with a bow and *arigato gozaimasu* (thank you) and it's over.

This is more like a warm-up than a lesson to learn a particular piece. When we've just gotten up and are not quite awake yet, the lessons wake us up. Whether the lesson is for *shamisen*, the *taiko* stick drum, the *tsuzumi* hand drum, or for dance, it is the same. Even with a dance that only lasts about twenty minutes, the lessons might continue over the space of a year. The lesson is for physical training so that it is not so important to remember the entire dance itself.

Professional dance teachers go to lessons too, but approach them in a very different way. People who teach dance go for their own lessons with an important teacher. For these people, who want to learn as many pieces as possible, spending an entire year on one twenty-minute piece is a waste of time. They need to learn a dance and remember its choreography as quickly as possible. For a professional dance teacher, a twenty-minute dance takes about a month, or at most two months, to learn. After they learn the dance they can then teach it to their own students. As actors we are trained to remember dance movements quickly and accurately and are often told that we must be able to remember a portion of a dance in three lessons.

But we actors do not particularly make our living from dance, so we have the leisure to gradually learn a dance over the course of a year.

A kabuki production is divided into a matinee program and an evening program with three items on each program. Each production runs for twenty-five days. At the Kabuki-za the matinee program begins at eleven or eleven-thirty and ends at three or three-thirty. There are very few actors that appear in all three plays, most appearing in two out of the three plays. Many actors use the time between the plays they appear in for additional lessons or practice.

An actor will say, "I'm going to a dance lesson," and then rush to a nearby studio and have a lesson. In the traditional teaching system there is usually no set schedule for lessons and students simply go in the order they arrive. The dance teachers understand the actor's situation, so they might say something to the other waiting students like, "Matazo has to go on soon. Do you mind if he goes first?" Many dance teachers live close to Ginza where the Kabuki-za is located. This way an actor can take the subway a couple of stops, have a proper fifteen- or twenty-minute lesson, and get back to the theater without taking more than an hour. This is the kind of life that actors lead—squeezing music and physical training lessons in between appearances on stage.

The evening program ends at about nine or nine-thirty. Many actors then go on for lessons after that on their way home. Some actors prefer evening lessons because in the morning they are worried about the day's performance and cannot concentrate. Morning lessons also mean that an actor has to be aware that he cannot be too leisurely about his lessons for fear of being delayed and leaving other actors in the lurch. After the performance, he can relax and concentrate on the lesson for as long as it takes.

After a night lesson it might be eleven or eleven-thirty by the time an actor gets home. Then he has to get up around eight the next morning, eat, go to his lessons and then go to the theater.

The twenty-five days of a kabuki run leaves five days of rehearsal for the following month's production; five days to learn all the lines and movements, although sometimes actors do start memorizing lines earlier. On occasion, when there is a new play, or a play that has not been done in a long time, rehearsals start earlier, around the twentieth of the preceding month.

IN THE DRESSING ROOM

The quietest time for an actor is from the middle to the end of a run. These are the days when an actor can relax the most. The period from the fifteenth to the twentieth has the fewest rehearsals and lessons. Actors can take care of their personal business at this time. During their private hours kabuki actors take off their kimonos and lead a modern life—drinking coffee, going for drives, etc.—just like other Japanese.

Kabuki actors have all kinds of hobbies. Some play with word processors and personal computers, there is even an actor with interest in astronomical observation. Ichimura Manjiro knows enough to be called "Professor Astronomy," and, as is fitting for the second son of Uzaemon, he is also an accomplished player of the *shamisen*. When I was in Brazil, thanks to Manjiro's advice, I was able to see Halley's comet from the top of a mountain.

An actor has until thirty minutes before the performance to check in by sticking a peg in the *chakutoban*. If he arrives after that, whether the performance has begun or not, he is counted as absent and a substitute goes on. Even fifteen minutes before curtain is too late and the actor is not allowed to go on. Afterwards the actor has to compensate the actor who went on in his place with money or some appropriate gift. Paying the stand-in is not the producer's responsibility. The burden has to be borne by the actor himself. Once I was unfortunate enough to be unable to go on stage for eight days and used up most of my paycheck for the month to compensate my stand-in.

From the instant we check in, everything we do naturally works to make us feel as though we are back in the Edo period (1603–1868). We change from Western clothing to cotton kimonos, and even change our underwear to *fundoshi* loincloths. No matter how you look at it kabuki belongs to the Edo period. All actors wear traditional loincloths. Over that goes the *juban* underrobe, and finally the cotton *yukata* kimono. In winter we wear wool kimonos and *haori* coats. By this time we are halfway into the Edo period. Afterwards, as we put on makeup, wigs, and costumes, the feeling becomes even stronger.

But kabuki actors are still men of the twentieth century. Just by entering the *gakuya* a person cannot be instantly transported to the Edo period. Gradually one starts to feel a part of a past world, but the process is much more difficult for people who normally wear modern clothes. I myself wear a traditional loincloth offstage, as well, to retain some of the mood of the world of Edo.

TEN MONTHS ON STAGE, TWO MONTHS OFF

In the old days theaters were closed in February and August, since these were the coldest and hottest months and audiences stayed away. During these two months actors lived on their savings. Now, though, if an actor wants to, he can work all twelve months of the year. Today theaters are air-conditioned and are comfortable in February and August so that plays can be put on. Also in July and August the Agency for Cultural Affairs sponsors tours that take kabuki to schools and auditoriums throughout Japan.

However, very few actors work all twelve months of the year. Most follow the practice of the past, working ten months and taking two off. That's probably because they need a break from the constant tension of daily performances.

Depending on their contracts, some actors are paid some of their regular salary during these breaks, while others have to live off their savings. There are very few actors who are paid even when they are not in a production, maybe fourteen or fifteen actors at most. Since there are about two hundred and sixty kabuki actors, that is only five percent of all kabuki actors that the production company values highly enough to give paid holidays.

If an actor wants to make outside appearances on television or in movies it is possible, but, in accordance with their contracts, this must be handled through the production company. Payments for these appearances go to the production company and then the production company pays us. In fact, relatively few kabuki actors want to appear on television, because television commitments can interfere with the schedule of stage appearances and the rotation of roles from month to month. Most, like myself, are not willing to exchange income from stage appearances for lower television fees and complicated negotiations about changes in a schedule that is decided about six months in advance.

PHYSICAL TRAINING

The most important thing for an actor is physical strength. Without physical endurance an actor cannot complete a performance. The life of kabuki actors with their strenuous schedule of regular performances is rather different from the lives of television entertainers, and many kabuki actors lead surprisingly Spartan and stoic lives. An actor whose physical strength declines will suffer the consequences on stage. This is true even for the actors in the smallest roles.

Kanjincho is a good example of a play which is a grueling test of endurance. When Matsumoto Koshiro VIII (1910–1982) played Benkei, I appeared as a retainer of Benkei's opponent Togashi Saemon. The roles of the men that Togashi has guarding the barrier of Ataka are true tests of endurance. From the beginning of the play until the moment that Togashi commands "Bring out the gifts!" a space of forty or forty-five minutes, they have to sit on stage in a *seiza* formal kneeling pose.

When Togashi gives his command they stand and carry trays of gifts, and until that instant they must sit as still as stone statues, not even blinking. Moving one's face or shifting one's legs is out of the question. If a supporting actor moves even a little, he will attract the audience's attention away from the main characters.

After handing over the gifts they return and sit *seiza* yet again, this time for another fifteen or twenty minutes. Playing these roles is torture. It is much more physically demanding than roles that require movement. I once played the role of Benkei in a recital. Benkei does not have to worry about his feet falling asleep, because he either stands or moves about in the center of the stage. Togashi sits on top of a round black lacquer barrel called a *katsura-oke* so that he has no problems with his legs going numb. Moreover he can expend his energy in a verbal sparring match with Benkei.

There is a role in this play even more painful than those of the barrier guards. That is the role of the child that holds Togashi's sword. He doesn't have a single line but just sits there the entire time that Togashi is on stage. The swordbearer is usually played by the son of a high ranking kabuki actor. However painful, this role is a way for the child to learn the play.

In kabuki, dances with lots of movement are relatively pleasant to perform. *Onnagata* female dances are painful. For *onnagata* dances one must pose, with legs slightly bent and weight lowered, and all one's energy goes into the tortuous task of holding these difficult positions. It is much easier to alternate between sitting and standing positions than to hold positions with both legs slightly bent, moving only to other equally difficult poses.

HEALTH MEASURES

Kabuki actors have to preserve their strength, so drinking is a real menace. The many actors who do drink find that a hot bath in the morning helps to alleviate the effects of alcohol. Even today, most Japanese prefer baths to showers, but the usual steaming hot Japanese bath is not usually taken until the end of the day.

A morning bath has other benefits as well, so even an actor who doesn't drink takes a morning bath. It loosens up the muscles, which is important before appearing on stage, especially if an actor is going to be part of a *tachimawari* fight scene. When you are turning somersaults from eleven in the morning, if your muscles aren't loosened up you risk serious injury.

It's important to warm one's voice up as well. It is said that the voice is in best shape about six hours after waking. So if you are appearing at noon, if you don't wake up at six, then once on stage your body will be awake but not your voice. For this reason I try to get up as early as possible and do vocal warm-ups in the morning.

Food also affects one's performance. A kabuki actor usually eats a very light lunch. If he eats a lot he'll get sleepy, and it might also be difficult to speak. If one's stomach is too full it becomes painful to project one's voice from the diaphragm. So usually actors just nibble on a sandwich or some noodles. It's best to eat a big breakfast and to have as light a lunch as possible. When an actor is playing a big role, over the course of the month he will generally lose from three to five kilograms.

For a particular production, the most difficult period is during the few days of rehearsal. After the play opens it is still quite demanding until the third or fourth day. By the time it reaches the middle of a month, no matter how painful it was at first, it becomes surprisingly easy, probably because one's body knows the role now. Whether it's a matter of long speeches, or strenuous dances or fight scenes, it no longer hurts and in fact becomes exhilarating.

When a production is over and there is nothing to do but sit around the house, it is easy to eat too much and get unfit. So the way I maintain my health is by practicing the lines from various plays and doing the proper amount of physical exercise.

They say that actors tend to live long lives. This could be because of the healthy alternation of extreme tension at the beginning of a production and total relaxation after it ends.

EXPRESSION AND MOVEMENT

Kabuki may seem very large and exaggerated, but in kabuki an actor must never exhaust his powers of expression at any one time. If you always speak as loudly as you can, you will ruin your voice and the audience will tire of you. If you have a certain total amount of energy then as a rule you should use about seventy percent and keep the remaining thirty percent in reserve for the few occasions when you really need it. In other words you must not try to shout everything, but hold back and reserve enough energy to keep a cool eye on yourself and control your performance.

At the same time that you are acting you always have to imagine that you are watching yourself on a television monitor. Even at the height of passion or when you are most absorbed in your role you must be able to preserve this cool eye. It is important for all actors to train themselves to have this capacity, not just kabuki actors. There is a story that once, when Charlie Chaplin was in the middle of a performance, he received a telegram saying that his father had died. Unable to control himself he burst into tears, but then rushed to the washroom in order to look at his face. In other words, at the same time that he was grieving, he wanted to see what that kind of face looked like.

Another story relates how the kabuki actor Kikugoro VI corrected his wife in the middle of a fight, saying, "Look how bad your posture is! If you're angry, you should raise your hand a little higher so it will look more like you're angry." This is the extent to which actors have trained themselves to always have another self watching their movements.

An actor must do this at all times, even when just riding the train or subway. A senior actor teaching a younger one will never fail to say something like, "Study the faces of the other people on the train. You don't pay enough attention, do you? Look closely at the guy across from you. Try to judge what kind of things he's thinking about. If you have no idea, then you don't have what it takes to be a good actor. In the instant that you pass by someone you should think about his age, what kind of work he might do and what he's thinking about at that moment."

This is easier said than done. It is especially difficult when someone is young. If one forces this detachment on a young actor who is not yet adequately trained, the result can be to rob his acting of its energy. When an actor is young, his energy is all he has; if you rob him of this, then all that is left is uninteresting acting.

So now, when teaching young people I've come to encourage them to act with all their energy at first, although this is something that is only possible much later, as I have found from my own experience. Developing the reserves of energy for a steady performance is probably something that can only be developed with long stage experience.

THE FACE

It is often said that it is not until the age of fifty that one really has a kabuki face. Now that I've reached the age of fifty I have come to believe that this is true. Until the last few years my face was only what I had received from my parents, it was not yet my own. As a person ages, his life is reflected in his face. A person who has suffered in poverty has this reflected in his face, while a person who has lived a life of leisure also has this reflected in his face. When a person reaches the age of fifty, the events of his life come to be reflected in his face. By the same token this means that by the age of fifty one's character is set—for better or worse, by the age of fifty it is pretty clear what roles one can and cannot play.

This is not a matter of acting skill, but something more fundamental. If roles were being allocated to a group of actors which included someone like myself and one of the young actors from an important acting family, the younger man would almost certainly be chosen for the role of the lord, and someone of my experience as a retainer. Similarly, the role of a young foot soldier would be given to an actor with yet other characteristics. Whatever costume is worn, experience, whether it comes from years on the stage in roles of increasing importance or from being born in kabuki, shows through.

After years of wearing costumes, I know how to make them fit perfectly. Also, for the past thirty years I've been using the same wig makers and wig dressers and they can now make wigs that fit my head perfectly without a single fitting. All I have to do is to pick up the telephone and say, "This time I'm playing a farmer," and they'll come up with a wig that is perfect. A young actor has to go and have his measurements taken for a wig, but even so, it is difficult to make it match perfectly. Somehow it just doesn't sit quite right. But after years of experience, even without special effort, the wigs seem to match up. This ability to make the wigs and costumes look right inevitably has its effect on our acting.

All actors find that when they are separated from the stage their bodies forget how to act. If an actor is out of shape and then suddenly tries to dance or do acrobatics, the results will be painful. Even when riding an escalator, instead of standing still an actor should walk, and if there are stairs, he should use them, keeping an eye on the escalator and keeping pace with it. Instead of using my subway pass all the way to the National Theater, I get off a stop early and take a twenty-minute walk to the theater. Even in the middle of daily life one should not forget to keep one's body in shape.

One cannot be too careful about one's voice. When an actor's voice cannot be heard his value drops immediately. As my teacher Mitsugoro said, "Voice comes first, then movement and then figure and bearing." So, even in daily life I am always careful to protect my throat. Sometimes if you shout too much your throat hurts and then your voice does not sound good. We say that the *choshi ga kuruu* (tuning is messed up). When this happens it is a big problem. If one appears on stage and only a little croak comes out, between the embarrassment and the complaints of the other actors, one ends up feeling that it would be better to not appear at all.

This is why we take extra care to see that such things don't happen. If an actor does happen to catch a cold, there are some traditional remedies for warding off the symptoms. They may sound rather awful, but they can save an actor from a lot of other problems: for a sore throat, put a little salt in your tea; and for a stuffed nose, make a rinse of salt and lukewarm water, inhale it in through the nose and spit it out through the mouth.

SPECIAL SKILLS

If an actor does not practice his artistic skills, whether in dance or the *taiko* stick drum or the *shamisen*, then his ability quickly declines. No matter how long an actor has been polishing his skills he continues to have lessons to be sure that he does not get rusty.

At the very least actors should study dance, *shamisen* and one of the instruments of the *hayashi* percussion ensemble: the *taiko* stick drum, the *tsuzumi* hand drum, or the noh flute. Star *onnagata* must also learn the *koto* zither and the *kokyu* which is a kind of bowed version of the shamisen. If an *onnagata* cannot play the *shamisen*, *koto* and *kokyu*, there are roles that they cannot play, so that they cannot let these lessons go.

In kabuki, unlike television, an actor really has to play his instrument. It cannot be done by a stand-in, and an actor without these artistic skills will not get the roles. This is one reason that actors take music lessons. And to study dance it is important to learn *shamisen*. If one can't play the *shamisen* then one doesn't have the proper sense of rhythm and can't dance well.

When it comes to vigorous dances like *Tomo Yakko*, which shows a samurai footman in the pleasure quarters, and *Echigo Jishi*, which shows a traveling performer of a lion dance, even the *shamisen* is not enough, one needs experience with the *taiko* stick drum as well. Both dances have difficult sections of rhythmical foot stamping, and for this, experience with the stick drum is vital. Unless you have actually played the music yourself you don't know what you have to do, or when to do it to produce the different kinds of sounds.

When I was in America teaching kabuki I saw some musicals on Broadway, and was impressed that on this point it is the same as kabuki. All the actors on stage were highly trained and disciplined. The same thing struck me recently in London as well.

If an actor cannot dance or play the drum or *shamisen*, he will never get a role that requires dancing. Even if there are no auditions, actors study with the same teachers so that the people who need to know have a very clear idea of everyone's abilities.

In addition there is the *nadai shiken*, the audition to obtain the rank of *nadai*. The other actors around us know how well an actor can dance, sing and play instruments. This makes the kabuki world very exacting, firmly rooted in the skills and practices of the Edo period.

The same cannot be said for the stage and television world. Even in period dramas, most of the actors have not had any of the proper training. Things may be getting better and there are now fewer people who are supposed to be playing the *shamisen* who are just going through the motions. However, to the trained musician, it is clear that there are many places where the motions do not match the sound. It is even worse with the hand drum.

There was a particularly bad example in a historical drama in which an actor taking the part of a warrior during the Warring States period was supposed to be playing the hand drum. Had he known anything about the instrument, it would have been clear that in the position he adopted it was absolutely impossible for that kind of sound to be produced. It was almost like holding a violin upside down and still pretending to play it. This is the kind of mistake that would be unthinkable today in a Japanese-produced Western-style drama, but passes without comment in a historical drama, perhaps because most of the audience members are also unfamiliar with traditional instruments.

We see the same kind of thing in television fight scenes. Sometimes I see television programs that forget the sliding step, and there will be a samurai, sword in scabbard, running along with his body jerking up and down because he is lifting his feet up high as he runs. The proper motion should be *suri ashi*, or "sliding step," a form of movement fundamental to Japanese martial arts as well as dance, that requires progress by sliding, often quite rapidly, forward, never lifting the feet from the ground.

If you have ever held a real sword, you would probably soon understand that the scene described above is impossibly unrealistic, and that no one would ever hold a sword and run that way. The cutting edge of a sword is an extremely fragile thing, and if you rattle it around inside the scabbard, the cutting edge will soon break off.

If one studies fencing or even the tea ceremony one will have lots of practice in *suri ashi*, but without such hobbies an actor probably would not realize that lifting the feet as one moves is alien to Japanese etiquette and deportment, and he may end up acting in ways that are physically inappropriate to the world depicted.

THE MODERN ORGANIZATION OF KABUKI

Until very recently in the world of kabuki there were no written contracts. With the exception of a few big stars, individual actors did not sign contracts with theaters or with producers.

It was not until 1961 that people in the kabuki world began to be aware of contracts. This was when Matsumoto Koshiro, along with some thirty other actors, moved from the Shochiku production company to the Toho production company. At that time Toho offered the group written contracts, including a provision that Toho would pay a percentage of our salaries in the months that we did not appear.

Another provision increased the pay of minor actors. At that time at Shochiku a monthly salary was 20,000 yen. Actors who signed with Toho would have their salaries increased to 25,000 yen. This was the first time that kabuki actors started paying attention to written contracts, and it is not so very long ago at all.

Until that time, even if an actor was bound to Shochiku, it was simply on the basis of an oral agreement. There was no written contract or legal proof of the arrangement. As far as the Shochiku producers were concerned, Danjuro was the only actor they really needed under contract, and it is possible that there might have been a written contract with Danjuro XI (1910–1965.) If there was a contract, it was probably very different from the ones we are familiar with today.

This is the way kabuki actors have always operated, so that when actors talk about contracts they are not entirely clear what is meant. This is not so surprising since, after all, as far as a kabuki actor is concerned, as long as there is work there is no particular need for a contract, and a verbal agreement will do. This is very different from the rest of the entertainment world.

The *deshi*, or actor's apprentice, is paid by the production company. The money is distributed by the teacher, at the beginning and end of a play in Toho's case, and the beginning and middle of the run in Shochiku's case. Beginning *deshi* get about 150,000 yen a month, plus certain allowances like travel expenses. Keeping in mind that everyone takes about two months of vacation per year, for which they do not receive salary, it is not easy to live as a young *deshi*. The actors also distribute small amounts of money to their *deshi* on about the fourteenth of the month as a kind of bonus. The actors also give out gifts to the wig dressers and prop men and all the technical staff involved with his role. This is a custom from the Edo period that has continued unchanged.

These gifts are an important source of income for the *deshi* and the technical staff, and in turn are a heavy responsibility for the actor. When I was a low-ranking actor in the third floor dressing room I was constantly told to strive for the day when I would be in a position to pay out such bonuses, and I looked forward to it.

There is a term, *senryo yakusha*, for a top star, a term meaning "thousand-gold-piece kabuki actor." This is a term that was popular in the Edo period and stems from the time that Ichikawa Danjuro appeared at the Ichimura-za and received a thousand *ryo* in gold, an enormous sum. But not even Danjuro could keep the thousand gold pieces all to himself. He would have had to distribute some of it to his *deshi*, his wig people, his costumer, and other technical staff, so that the amount that this *senryo yakusha* would have been left with was much less than a thousand gold pieces.

There is an immense range in actors' salaries, from the salaries of distinguished stars who are honored as Living National Treasures, to the salaries paid to younger popular stars and to the ranks of the humble supporting players. But no actor knows how much another actor is paid. It is management policy to keep this highly confidential, an effective technique used by both Shochiku and Toho. Management can always accompany a little favor with a remark that, "We're only doing this for you specially."

I first received a salary as an actor in 1962 as a contract player for Toho. The ordinary contract was 25,000 yen for a production. With a twenty-five day run, that comes to a thousand yen per day. I remember that even though I had no lines, I was overjoyed that I could finally be paid for acting.

At present, about ninety percent of major kabuki actors are with Shochiku. Most are not under exclusive contract, so they are only paid when they appear. One reason for this is that there was a time when Shochiku ran into financial difficulties because it had too many actors under exclusive contract, so it changed its system. Now one can say that most kabuki actors run their careers as individual businesses.

Matsumoto Koshiro was a pioneer in these developments. When Koshiro moved to Toho, he insisted on a written contract. In turn, major actors of his class like Bando Mitsugoro and Onoe Shoroku at Shochiku also demanded contracts.

Then, in 1976, Koshiro organized the Koshiro Jimusho. This company is what would be called an agency in the television world. It handles all the arrangements for appearances inside and outside of kabuki for both major actors and their *deshi*. Since the *deshi* must appear in the same place in order to assist their teacher, their arrangements must be handled together with his. Following Koshiro's example, other actors set up their own offices.

BIT PLAYERS

If an actor is not the heir of a famous kabuki family, he cannot rise above the rank of a third-floor actor unless he passes the *nadai shiken* (test for the rank of *nadai*.) A "third-floor" actor means the same thing as an actor who is in the collective dressing room in films. In other words it means, "all the others." In kabuki they are called "third-floor" actors because of the way that kabuki dressing rooms are traditionally built, with the big collective dressing room on the third floor.

Third-floor actors' names do not appear on the sign board outside the theater. Actors who have passed the *nadai shiken* appear on the *iori* signboard, which is the sign displayed under a roof during the annual *kaomise* production. The names from Danjuro on down through all the *nadai* who have passed the test are listed, all in a row.

But the third-floor actors are not listed. None of the people doing acrobatics in fight scenes, none of the actors playing passersby are listed on the bill. Until very recently, they did not appear on the printed program distributed inside the theater, either. There is, however, a practical reason for this. While stars know what roles they are going to play well in advance, a *deshi* only knows what theater he is appearing in and usually does not know what roles he will play until the last minute. This means that the *deshi* must always be trained and prepared for all the small roles in kabuki. But this also means that it is difficult to print a program in time for opening day with all the right names for all the roles.

The difference between *nadai* actors and third-floor actors is more absolute than people outside the kabuki world might ever guess. I know this from my personal experience during the years that I spent as a third-floor actor.

Even though their names do not appear on the bill, this does not mean that these actors do not have acting names. Sometimes their teachers give them very whimsical names. For example, there are acting names like Usagi (rabbit) and Komori (bat). Many *deshi* of Ennosuke (whose name includes the character for monkey) have animal names.

Among the third-floor actors we must also include experienced senior actors like the late Bando Yaenosuke (1909–1986), who was recognized by the Japanese government as a Living National Treasure. He was the greatest choreographer of acrobatics and fight scenes in recent history, but he was not very good at delivering lines, so he never attained *nadai* rank, even though he was a Living National Treasure.

Yaenosuke could still execute proper *tombo* flips at the age of seventy and was one of the most important teachers in the National Theater training program. Matagoro, too might say "This is how you do a *tombo* flip," and then shock the students by doing it. Unless you can impress the students by backing up your words with action, young people will not listen.

THE RANK OF NADAI

To return to the topic at hand, when an actor passes the *nadai shiken*, the scale of his salary goes up dramatically. In my own case, it increased five times. But much of this increase slips away with increased expenses. When an actor becomes *nadai*, his dressing room changes; the costumer comes to his dressing room to put the costume on; the wig dresser also comes and puts on the wig. In return, at the middle of the month one has to show one's appreciation with some money in an envelope for each of them. It feels good finally to be in a position to do this, but it is a burden all the same.

It is not only the costumer and the wig dresser who receive envelopes either. One also has to tip the prop master and the old man who opens and closes the little curtain at the end of the *hanamichi* with a smart clatter of curtain rings when one makes entrances and exits. And, of course, one has to give a little something to the man who greets you at the dressing room door and is always ready with your own slippers to exchange for your street shoes.

Even though my pay went up to 100,000 yen, nearly a third of that went to reward the backstage staff who helped me directly, so in reality, my salary did not go up all that much. Now I understand what a strain it must have been to be a *senryo yakusha* like Danjuro in the Edo period.

KOKEN AND DESHI

Koken are the stage assistants, sometimes dressed all in black and sometimes dressed in formal costume. They help an actor with his costume or take care of hand props when needed. These *koken* are always *deshi* of the actor that they assist.

So when you watch kabuki, it is safe to guess that the *koken* assisting Danjuro as he dances is a *deshi* of Danjuro, or that the koken at the back of the stage who wipes the sweat off Koshiro's face when he dances Benkei in *Kanjincho,* or hands Benkei his rosary is a *deshi* of Koshiro.

Originally *deshi* had to be capable of stepping in smoothly in the case of an emergency, for example, standing in for actors if they suddenly collapsed on stage or prompting one if he forgot his lines. Elderly actors find it increasingly difficult to remember things they have memorized. At those times the *koken* should be crouching unobtrusively nearby to whisper the lines to the actor. Thus the *koken* has a position of great responsibility.

In fact, there have been many famous kabuki actors who have had trouble remembering their lines. One of these actors was Nakamura Nakazo I (1736–1790) who later became immensely famous.

He was once in a play in which he was supposed to enter and very quickly announce, "My lord, this is my report! General So-and-so has attacked my lord's forces at such-and-such a place!" He no sooner shouted, "My lord, this is my report!" than he realized that he had no idea what came next.

Without a second thought, he approached the star playing the lord and whispered, "I'm sorry, I've forgotten the line." The lord then grunted his assent and said, "I understand. Thank you for your report," and the play went on. Afterwards, Nakazo was sure he would be reprimanded but instead the star said "Well done," and gave him some money as a reward. They say that this was the beginning of Nakazo's rise as an actor.

As a rule, the roles of retainers who come on and say, "My lord, this is my report,"—and there are many such roles—are played by low-ranking actors from the collective dressing room. I've played these roles many, many times. They are actually quite difficult because you have to run on along the *hanamichi,* stop short near the stage and announce your lines in a loud voice. The *hanamichi* is long and it is difficult to have enough breath left after running to deliver your lines.

On top of that, since you are still on the *hanamichi* running through the audience, when you stop to say your lines, the faces of the audience are right before your eyes, so that it is easy to get stage fright and be unable to force your voice out. At worst, you forget your lines entirely in this situation. In that case you just stand there silently, eyes staring wide. The expression for this among actors is *dango o kuu* which means "eating your dumplings."

Also, no matter how great an actor is, he can't win against the process of aging, so there are times when an older actor forgets his lines entirely, and has to be prompted a great deal. When this happens it is very sad, but it can happen to the best actors.

By and large, though, it is unusual for an actor to forget his lines. But to be ready for any situation, the *koken* must know by heart the lines of the actor that he is assisting. This is a form of training as well because the *koken* memorizes the play this way and learns the meaning of obscure lines.

For example, there are lines that Benkei says in *Kanjincho* that I did not understand just watching from the audience, and it was only after being immersed in the play that I understood them. This understanding came from being a *koken* and playing the role of one of Togashi's retainers, that difficult sitting role I mentioned earlier.

Even though I talk about memorizing lines, in the old days, in the late seventeenth and early eighteenth centuries when the classical repertory was first being performed, there were no written scripts such as we have today. Each actor learned a role from some master actor and wrote out his own lines by brush. This is the material he had to refer to to learn his role.

Originally, Benkei would only know Benkei's lines and Togashi would only know Togashi's lines. They would not be shown the lines of other characters. So when it came to the first read throughs, it must have been difficult because even if an actor knew his own lines, he had no idea what the actor with whom he was having a dialogue would say. The playwright would indicate who was supposed to speak next and so gradually an actor learned his cues as well.

An actor who only had one or two words at a time might say his line and then think, "Fine, now that's over with," and not pay any more attention. Even today there are many plays like this. However, with newly written kabuki plays, especially plays influenced by Western realism, this kind of attitude would be a problem. This is one reason that newly written plays tend to have full scripts with all the characters' lines written out.

The traditional method for learning lines, such as those of Benkei, was to carefully observe someone playing Benkei several times. And in this way, kabuki has been preserved for hundreds of years. Because actors must watch and remember every line of standard plays like *Kanjincho*, there isn't a single actor in the kabuki world that does not know every line. It has been indelibly imprinted on their memories through constant repetition.

Both because actors' powers of memory have been finely honed and because they probably know the lines of the standard repertory, even at the first reading the actors are assumed to have memorized all their lines. An actor who does not know his lines will be embarrassed, and be ridiculed or scolded by the other actors. It is an actor's responsibility to memorize quickly, or if it is a play that you are unfamiliar with, to consult some senior actor who knows about the proper way to perform the role.

A person who is a *koken* must be able to do both what the actor does and what the *koken* does. Also, his timing must be perfectly coordinated with the actor he works with. This is why they must be the actor's own *deshi*, who are constantly with him in the theater and accustomed to his every idiosyncrasy.

When a person sees kabuki for the first time and sees these *koken* on stage, he may think that they get in the way of the real action. But the *koken* are also actors playing roles on stage that are absolutely vital. A kabuki performance is a ceremony in which *koken* are indispensable participants.

SETS AND PROPS

Just as kabuki preserves a world different from modern daily life, there is a corner of the kabuki world that is different from the rest. Modern Japanese don't like tattoos much, even the florid masterpieces of craftsmanship that are so admired abroad. Here they are immediately associated with gangsters and violent manual laborers. In the kabuki world, though, among the stage hands, you might find some concealing a tattoo. Tattooing is an agonizing process performed by inserting tiny amounts of coloring under the skin, inducing great pain. Those who have been tattooed pride themselves on their endurance and constantly challenge each other, perhaps with feats of moxabustion, a

medical technique that involves burning small amounts of a
sage-like grass on acupuncture points, or by being tattooed more
and more elaborately.

In the Edo period some actors were tattooed. It was a sign of
machismo, but there another justification. The tattooing process was thought to be a kind of health treatment. When the coloring, especially the red coloring, is applied it causes a high
fever. This fever was thought to be a good treatment for
venereal disease. So at the time, men who frequented the
brothels in Yoshiwara might also go and be tattooed for safety's
sake. These tattoos were different from the ones that convicted
criminals were branded with, for after all, they were done
because the people wanted them.

Sets for kabuki have been made by a shop run for generations
by the Hasegawa family. From the shop of the Edo period to the
modern company Kanai Odogu, it has continued as the same
firm, with the name Hasegawa Kambei being bestowed on its
head in the same way that honored names are given to actors.

These days set workers all wear blue jeans, but until recently
they wore black knickerbocker-like pants called *tatetsuki-
bakama*, black *hanten* coats and *zori* sandals. There used to be
large numbers of workers dressed like this working for Kanai
Odogu.

In Japanese, sets are called *odogu*, meaning "big tools," and
props are called *kodogu*, meaning "little tools." The division between costumes, sets, and props is extremely complex and
depends on confusing traditions about what belongs to whom,
but for general purposes, if you think that anything that doesn't
move is a set, while things that are moved are props, you will not
be far wrong. Kabuki sets are handled by Kanai Odogu, and in
the same way, there is a special company for kabuki props, Fujinami Kodogu.

Fujinami Kodogu was established in the Meiji period by a
man named Fujinami Yohei. Even though it is now organized as
a modern company, it continues to be headed by a holder of the
Fujinami Yohei name. This company handles the rental and
handling of all the props used for productions of kabuki at the
Kabuki-za and the National Theater. The company handles
some props for television as well.

It would be extremely expensive to keep these things on hand or to buy them new. For example, think of the expense of making the kind of fancy brazier used by a high ranking samurai lord, one set up on four legs, each time one is needed. Imagine how troublesome it would be to get just the kind of decorated screen that might be used in the home of a commoner in the Edo period.

In both television and films, any story set in the Edo period takes its standard from props for kabuki. For example, the swords used these days for samurai dramas are now made from aluminum alloys so that they can be produced cheaply, but their shape is based on that of kabuki prop swords (which are now made of bamboo). There are also companies producing wigs and costumes that have continued from generation to generation in the same way as sets and props. For ages these firms have been supported by the patronage of the kabuki theater, and in turn they support the kabuki theater and allow it to continue by providing whatever is needed for stage productions.

Among the items handled by the prop people are the *zori* straw sandals worn by so many of the characters on the kabuki stage. However, the cost of the *waraji* straw that goes into *zori* is now so high that it has become a problem for the prop company. So now, instead of pure straw, plastic is also used, especially for the thongs that hold the sandals on. Plastic is good for that purpose because it is very strong. In fact, sometimes it is too strong.

In a play called *Megumi no Kenka*, which is about clashes between teams of firefighters in the Edo period, there is a scene where one of the firefighters comes running on and the string on his *zori* breaks. He then breaks off a length of *waraji* string and reties it. That is impossible with the tough plastic *zori*.

On this one occasion real *waraji* is used. In the old days there was no problem because *zori* sandals were everyday footwear and there were large numbers of craftsmen twisting *waraji* into sandals. Now the craftsmen are all gone so the cost of *waraji* has gone up tremendously and a pair of real *zori* costs about 5,000 yen, the same as a normal pair of shoes. Plastic *zori* only cost a few hundred yen. The fact that they can't be used on all occasions must be a real headache for the propman.

The paper umbrella is another once easily obtainable prop that is now expensive. A modern metal and cloth umbrella can be had for about a thousand yen; a paper one made by traditional methods costs many times that. One of the highlights of the play *Shiranami Gonin Otoko,* which is about the careers of five thieves, is a scene when all five starring actors line up on stage in lavish matching kimono holding matching paper umbrellas, each with the word *shiranami* or "white wave," a term meaning thief, written boldly on it. The scene is spectacular, but the expense of replacing those umbrellas regularly is always increasing.

Costumers have similar problems. The natural vegetable dyes that create the colors needed for kimono patterns are no longer available. It seems that it has become extremely difficult to obtain the plants from which the dyes are made in Japan. Synthetic pigments give harsh and unacceptable colors. Green is the worst—the modern color is extremely strong and the more gentle hue of the past seems to be impossible to recreate. Yet if you tried to use only vegetable dyes and maintain the colors of the past, the expense would be horrendous.

For these economic reasons, the costumes and props of kabuki keep changing little by little. It is unavoidable. When people say that the kabuki of today is not the kabuki of the past, they are only thinking of the way that the acting has changed from the acting that they remember from the past. If you ask kabuki actors, you will find that there are many aspects of kabuki other than acting that have changed as well.

There is no one in particular to blame for this. While we work to preserve the plays of the great tradition of kabuki, the plays of the *juhachiban* collection for example, many other things will change no matter what we do.

Actors have also changed physically. The two sons of Matsumoto Hakuo, Matsumoto Koshiro and Nakamura Kichiemon, are both very tall, almost six feet. When an actor is that tall, if you put a wig and tall court cap on him the hat scrapes the top of the doorways. Tall actors have to stoop when making their entrances, and this can change the effect entirely. For example, in the *Ga no Iwai* scene from *Sugawara Denju Tenarai Kagami,* there is a famous moment when Sakuramaru enters through the upstage doorway. He has decided that the only way he can atone for his errors is to commit *seppuku* ritual suicide. This determination is communicated by the calm way that he slips through the *noren* curtain into the room. If he has to bend down to get through the doorway, the effect is more like a man shuffling in with a delivery of noodles, so the doorway has had to be made larger than it was in the past.

There is the same problem in *Sukeroku*. In one scene the henchmen of the villain Ikkyu sit on a line of benches to one side of the stage. They are a magnificent sight, all in handsome cotton kimono with bold patterns and wearing *geta* clogs. Unfortunately, Japanese are larger than they were in the past and it is a strain to sit on these low benches for over an hour. To make it more comfortable, the benches need to be made about six centimeters higher. But if the props people are asked to do something like that, the response will be something like: "We've been doing this since the Edo period and there haven't been benches with measurements like that in three hundred years of kabuki." Kabuki actors solve the problem by putting a small box on top and sitting on that.

As the bodies of actors have changed, so no doubt eventually the props will have to change as well. In the days that the forms of these props were originally set, actors were shorter and smaller. No matter how much one wants to maintain tradition, using the same measurements as in the Edo period may cause insurmountable problems, and while the people in charge of sets, props, wigs and costumes all work to preserve the ways of doing things that have been passed down from the Edo period, some changes will be unavoidable.

SUPERSTITIONS

Superstitions are strongly held among the people of the kabuki world. In the famous ghost play *Tokaido Yotsuya Kaidan* a woman named Oiwa is given a poison that disfigures her horribly and leads to her death. During the play, her ghost appears in various forms to take vengeance on her enemies. This play is distantly based on a true story and there is a shrine in Tokyo dedicated to Oiwa-sama. Whenever a production of *Yotsuya Kaidan* is planned, the actors pay their respects at the shrine without fail. In 1965 when Matagoro played Oiwa-sama, we all went to Oiwa-sama's shrine in Yotsuya.

While we were there we heard the sound of a baby crying in a house behind the shrine. This gave us all a start because one of the most dramatic scenes of the play is punctuated by the pitiful cry of Oiwa-sama's baby. It seems that this shrine is supervised by the descendants of Oiwa-sama herself. We offered *sake* in remembrance of Oiwa-sama, and her descendants accepted our offerings.

We refer to the woman as Oiwa-*sama*, and the shrine as Yotsuya-*san*. "Sama" and "san" are both terms of great respect and no one involved with kabuki would ever off-handedly say "Oiwa," or refer to the Inari shrine that presides over the entrance to the dressing room simply as "Inari." There is no telling what would result from speaking Oiwa-sama's name disrespectfully.

There are also many stories of strange happenings associated with certain theaters. I won't mention the name, but there is a certain theater with a distinguished history dating back to the Meiji period that is famous among actors as a place where many strange things happened. This theater burned down in the Great Kanto Earthquake of 1923, and burned down again in World War II. They say that the spirits of the many actors that died there during the earthquake and wartime bombing occupy the rebuilt theater, unable to find peace, and perhaps this is why actors believe that in the passageway under the *hanamichi*, a place appropriately called the *naraku* or "hell," strange voices can be heard coming from below. There are those who say that a place like a theater dressing room is a common place for spirits to linger. In any case there is something weird about this theater.

Once while I was appearing at the theater, one of my fellow actors in the *obeya* committed suicide. He was an older actor who was regarded affectionately by all of us. He sat at the mirror two over from me so that we often had opportunities to chat. One day without warning he did not appear in the dressing room. Quickly we found someone to stand in for him. Strangely enough, even after a week he didn't reappear. Thinking that this was odd, someone went to check the room near the theater where he lived and found his decaying body. He had hanged himself. In order to make it convenient to go to the theater he lived apart from his family and there was no one living close to him. This is probably why it took so long to discover his body.

The story begins at this point. Several days after the funeral, a *deshi* of this actor made a bad joke. Just as the performance began he brought in some incense that he had borrowed from the prop man—there are so many death scenes in kabuki that there is no shortage of utensils for prayers for the dead—altars, prayer bells, and incense. He went to the mirror that the dead actor had used and said, half in jest, "This was where he sat, wasn't it. The poor thing. Here, let me burn some incense for him." The other actors joined in the spirit and, also half in jest, enthusiastically burned incense and rang prayer bells. The spirit of the kabuki *mono* lives on. There is still something in a kabuki actor that allows him to do things unthinkable in the everyday world.

Anyway, when that *deshi* returned from appearing on stage, he found that the cushion at the mirror where the old actor sat was soaking wet, as though someone had emptied a glass of water on it. Everyone immediately thought that this was the old actor's tears. It had only been about thirty or forty minutes from the time that the actors mirthfully prayed in jest, went out on stage and returned. The *deshi* who had started things was not the only one to turn pale. This time all of the actors in the dressing room prayed for the old actor in great seriousness. The incident reminded us all of how frightening this theater can be.

Countless people have said that they have heard something in the *obeya* dressing room or the *naraku* passageway. Even important kabuki stars pray whenever they have to go through the *naraku* passageway. Just recently, an actor told me, "When I was going through the *naraku* there was something sitting there blocking the passageway. I had no choice, so I straddled it and went on through." The only way to get from the stage to the entrance to the *hanamichi* is by going through the dimly-lit *naraku* passageway that runs from underneath the stage to the *agemaku* curtain at the end of the *hanamichi*. What else could the actor do when he encountered something sitting right in the middle of the passageway? He clasped his hands in prayer and hurried on, passing by whatever it was as he went. He had to, because otherwise he'd be late for his entrance. Ghosts are frightening enough, but an actor with the nerve to straddle a ghost in order to make an entrance is even scarier.

CHAPTER 6

Kabuki's Audience

What kind of people go to see kabuki today? A look at the audience will reveal, not very surprisingly, that most are older people and that the audience is overwhelmingly female. Of course these are the people who have enough time to spend an entire day at the theater. Also, most people do not go as individuals, but as members of groups so that the kabuki theater is nearly always full with large sections taken up by various groups such as organizations of school alumni, people affiliated with a particular company or perhaps a particular regional government.

On almost any performance day you will see a desk out in front of the Kabuki-za with a sign welcoming the particular group and handing out bags containing programs, presents and other items that commemorate their visit and make it more pleasant. While it is good that so many people are going to see kabuki, it is too bad that more of them do not go to enjoy the performance for itself, rather than out of a sense of obligation to a particular group.

It is difficult for most people to go see kabuki regularly since tickets, like everything else in Japan, are quite expensive. The best seats at the Kabuki-za cost over 10,000 yen while the best seats at the National Theater are about 8,000 yen. The cheapest seats are around 2,000 yen and there are student discounts at the National Theater. There are no standing room tickets, but at the Kabuki-za it is possible to get tickets to see a single section of a long program. Every month there is a new schedule of

113

prices based on the length of each section, and people who buy these tickets walk up a long flight of stairs that is separated from the main theater to a section of seats at the very top of the third-floor balcony.

Today, aside from a few special features, the public area of a kabuki theater differs very little from Western theaters. When you walk into the lobby there are the usual ushers and stalls selling programs and memorabilia. There are also stalls renting out opera glasses and stalls renting little earphone receivers through which one can hear commentaries on the plays in Japanese or English.

One unusual feature is that there are many restaurants inside the theater. Since a complete program lasts over four hours, there is always one long intermission to allow people to eat. Some people bring their own lunch boxes, others rush to reserve a place and order a meal as soon as they get into the theater.

The stalls and restaurants may seem to be merely services provided by the theater, but in the Edo period, the theater teahouses that surrounded a theater served a very important function. Audience members would buy their tickets from the teahouse and then would sit in a special section inside the theater reserved for patrons of that teahouse decorated with lanterns bearing the teahouse's name. Even today, the front of the balcony is decorated with lanterns, a reminder of the old days. The teahouse might have brought food and drink to their patrons, or the patrons could withdraw to the teahouse to eat or perhaps to change their clothing. In the old days, these teahouses were so important that often they were a major source of financial backing for the play producers. Today there are no more theater teahouses, but groups continue to be an important part of the kabuki audience.

Inside the auditorium most of the seating is Western-style. The Kabuki-za seats 2,600 and the large hall at the National Theater seats 1,746. This is much larger than Edo-period theaters which were closer in size to the small hall at the National Theater, which seats 630. The sizes of the Edo-period stage and the small hall's stage are also comparable. But even though the stage is the same size, the Edo-period theaters probably squeezed more people into the audience since the theater was divided into boxes which held several people, much like the box seating at a sumo wrestling match today.

On either side of the auditorium there are box seats called *sajiki* which face the audience directly. Despite the fact that the view is not very good from these seats, they are the most expensive. Part of the reason is that they are more comfortable because you can stretch out, and have tea and food set out in front of you, and part of the reason is that you can be seen by the rest of the audience. This is especially nice at the *kaomise* performance in Kyoto because the *sajiki* seats are filled with the Kyoto geisha called *maiko*, faces white with makeup and and wearing lavish kimono and hair ornaments. Actors appreciate the *sajiki* because it means that there are audience members on every side. At the National Theater the seating is entirely Western style and there are no *sajiki*, instead there are blank walls on either side of the auditorium, which feels a little bit lonely compared to the Kabuki-za.

Compared with most Western theaters, the auditorium is very wide, but not very deep. The stage is wide, but even though there are two balconies, no seat is very far from it. You have to be close to the actors to appreciate their acting, for as large and exaggerated as kabuki acting seems, the impression of size is created by small flourishes that can't be seen from far away.

Where are the best seats for watching kabuki? Front row seats are closest to the stage, but have no other advantage. They are called "sand-covered" seats, and in some of the worse theaters they are in fact covered in dirt. An actor delivering his lines with great force can also deliver quite a shower of saliva—Mitsugoro was notorious for this—and much of this also ends up in the front row. From this close up you can see the actors sweat, which ruins much of their attractiveness. The best seats are in the fifth to the tenth rows.

HISTORY IN KABUKI PLAYS

In order to appreciate kabuki, a certain amount of background knowledge is necessary. Of course, this is true for the appreciation of any art form. Having this basic knowledge or not can leave you with an entirely different impression and affect the value you derive from having been to a performance.

First, it is necessary to understand that there are many plays in which the characters and the period are very different from the historical incidents on which they are based. This is a device forced on kabuki playwrights by the repressive policies of the Edo-period shogunate. Unlike the fortunate times in which we now live, in the Edo period freedom of expression was almost totally denied, and punishment for those who fell foul of the authorities was extreme—including sentences such as being put into manacles for several days, several months in prison, or a demolishment order on the offender's home.

In the theater, who could perform and what kind of material could be used (it was forbidden to present on the stage any event that had attracted public attention, particularly one involving members of the samurai class) were so strictly regulated that in order to avoid the censors who could ban plays and have their authors thrown into prison, playwrights disguised their plots as events taking place in some other era and their characters with fictitious names.

The play *Chushingura* is a good example of this. The actual event, a revenge against their former lord's persecutor and ritual suicide by forty-seven loyal retainers, occurred in 1702 and the sensational story had all the right ingredients for the kind of drama enjoyed by the common people of Edo. But the playwrights knew that keeping faithfully to the details could only end in the production being banned and themselves being punished. For this reason, although many people then and now know the origin of the events depicted in the play, *Chushingura* is set some four hundred years earlier, in the Kamakura period, with a cast of fictitiously named characters. Without knowledge of this background, no modern audience can follow the story as it is presented on the kabuki stage.

Popular demand also gave rise to plays presented as historical drama. For instance, the people of the Edo period were fascinated by stories of the deeds of twelfth-century leader of the Genji clan, Minamoto Yoshitsune, and the playwrights did not hesitate to satisfy their appetite for plays, however contrived, with Yoshitsune as the hero.

Similar considerations affect not only period plays but also domestic dramas. By keeping these points in mind enjoyment of a kabuki performance will be far greater than if one tries to relate the action on stage to actual history.

The kabuki ideal is for the actors to be as physically close to the audience as possible, although today, as in the Western theater, there is a proscenium frame around the stage separating it from the audience and framing it like a picture. In the Edo period, the stage stuck out into the audience and there were people on the stage watching. Of course, there is the *hanamichi* runway, an integral part of kabuki since its beginnings, that goes right through the audience and is an extension of the stage, bringing the action right into the middle of the audience. Unfortunately, at the Kabuki-za, in order to bring the third-floor balcony as close to the main stage as possible, the builders of the theater blocked off the view of the *hanamichi* so that from the cheaper seats, much of the action is totally invisible. But when the actor Ichikawa Ennosuke performs his *chunori*, flying through the air above the hanamichi, he goes all the way to the third floor balcony, so this is the one chance that people up there have to see a dramatic exit.

YAGO AND KAKEGOE

The third-floor balcony is also the home of the *omuko* or men who shout during the performance. *Omuko* means "the ones across the way," which probably comes from the fact that they are usually in the back of the theater. In the Edo period everyone shouted their approval of the acting, but doing this just right is difficult and is mostly done by specialists. Some people think that they are paid by the theater, but they are actually amateurs who love kabuki and are organized into clubs and receive passes that allow them into the third-floor balcony for free, where they enliven the atmosphere of the theater.

This is a sound that is inextricably associated with the experience of watching kabuki. When a scene reaches its climax, you will hear shouts of "Otowa-ya!" or "Narita-ya!" from the audience. These shouts are called *kakegoe*. All Japanese immediately think, "Ah, now that is kabuki," the instant they hear this sound. Shouting *kakegoe* is a custom peculiar to the kabuki theater.

The words that they shout, "Otowa-ya" or "Narita-ya" are

called *yago*. When *yago* originated the social standing of actors was extremely low. There may have been actors receiving a thousand gold pieces as their salary, but from the standpoint of respectable society, actors were so low in status that they were outside and below the four accepted classes of samurai, farmer, craftsman, merchant, in descending order.

Kabuki actors wanted to do what they could to try to climb out of such a degrading situation. They could not have hoped to approach the standing of a samurai lord, but at least wanted the same respectability as a grocer, or dry-goods merchant or even fishmonger, members in good standing in the four-class system.

"Otowa-ya," or "Echigo-ya" sound like the names of the shops of merchants, because many merchants in Edo named their shops after the places they came from. Kabuki actors imitated this custom. Instead of having audience members shout something like "Matazo!," if they shout "Harima-ya!" then at least an actor has something like the status of a merchant. This was a very welcome thing to an actor since it meant that, at least while he was on stage, he had the same standing as the other commoners.

In later times, after Danjuro IX arranged for the emperor to see kabuki, thereby raising the status of actors, the *kakegoe* changed into a form of applause for an actor. Either way, we would never want the audience to abandon this custom.

One reason actors like to have people shout *kakegoe* is that for that one instant, the actor can take a breath. In other words, a *kakegoe* often comes about three-quarters of the way through a climactic line. An actor can use all his breath for the first part of the line and then use the pause created by the *kakegoe* to take a big breath and give power to the end of the line.

The effect is ruined if the timing of the *kakegoe* is off. It is wonderful when the timing is on; if it's off by just a little, instead of allowing the actor to take a breath and give power to his speech, the effect will be exactly the opposite. The actor won't be able to take a breath at all. It is difficult to explain the timing, but in any case we actors want all the well-timed *kakegoe* that we can get. They are a big help, encouraging us and giving us the breath that we need to go on.

Vaious *yago* indicate different groups in the world of kabuki. I belong to the Harima-ya group. There are many other actors within the Harima-ya group. Probably the most famous bearer of the *yago* Harima-ya was Nakamura Kichiemon I (1886–1954), who was referred to as "Oharima." Another member is my teacher Nakamura Matagoro, or "Mata Harima."

To see how these *yago* indicate families of actors, let's look at a few of the lines of leading men. The *yago* of the Ichikawa line, the single most prestigious line in kabuki, is "Narita-ya." For generations members of the Ichikawa family have been believers in the shrine to Fudo at Narita, which is the reason for this *yago*. The shrine is close to Tokyo's International Airport. In return for the Ichikawa line's patronage, the shrine has supported generations of the Ichikawa family.

Originally the word *yakusha*, which is used for kabuki actors, referred to a shaman who acted as an intermediary between men and Shinto divinities. Perhaps by serving the Narita Fudo the Ichikawa family is following the true vocation of a *yakusha*. The Danjuro line is known for *aragoto*, and often an *aragoto* hero is a kind of superhuman semi-divine figure. On occasion, a Danjuro appeared on stage as the god Fudo. One way of looking at the *yago* is to think of Narita-ya as a shop that specializes in *aragoto*.

Imagine walking down the street a bit. Next door is a shop called Korai-ya. Narita-ya, in this case Danjuro XI (1910–1965), had a younger brother named Matsumoto Hakuo (1910–1982), better known by his earlier name of Koshiro VIII, and Korai-ya is the *yago* of the Matsumoto line. The present holder of the name is Koshiro IX. The Ichikawa and Matsumoto families have always been closely related, and the name Koshiro is almost as important as the name Danjuro. From the eighteenth century the name Koshiro has been especially important as the name of actors playing dashing villains. As the name for a leading man, Koshiro rivals Danjuro.

The present Koshiro also has a younger brother named Nakamura Kichiemon II, Harima-ya, and the two brothers have a healthy rivalry. In the same way that in a merchant firm an heir might be adopted to keep the store going if there is no appropriate son, Kichiemon has been adopted as the heir to his mother's father, Kichiemon I (1886–1954). If Narita-ya and

Korai-ya have traditions going back centuries, Harima-ya is a twentieth-century tradition since the first Kichiemon was probably the greatest actor of historical plays of this century. This is what the Harima-ya sells and the *yago* comes from the fact that the first holder of the name was from Harima, which is the old name for a part of Hyogo Prefecture in Kansai.

Across the street is Narikoma-ya. This is the *yago* of Nakamura Utaemon, which specializes in *onnagata*. Somewhere along the line one group split off so that there is also a separate Narikoma-ya group which is connected to Osaka and Kyoto. This group is represented by Nakamura Senjaku II (soon to take the name Ganjiro III) and his father, the late Nakamura Ganjiro II (1902–1983). This line preserves the Kansai tradition of acting, especially in the domestic plays of Chikamatsu Monzaemon. Both Ganjiro II and Senjaku are famous for their performances as the weak but attractive young men that are the protagonists of so many of these plays. Senjaku is also famous as an *onnagata*—nowadays it is not unusual for actors to play both male and female roles.

The first holder of the name Ganjiro was a *deshi* of an earlier Utaemon and that is why the two groups have the same *yago*. In other words, there are two branches of Narikoma-ya, the Tokyo branch centered around Utaemon and the Kansai branch centering around Ganjiro and Senjaku and including the actor Hayashi Yoichi.

My own acting name Nakamura is also distantly related to the Utaemon line since the first Kichiemon descended from a *deshi* of an Utaemon. My teacher Matagoro's father was Matagoro I (1885–1920) and he was a close friend of the late Ganjiro II. And at the beginning of their careers they were *deshi* together. Nearly everyone in the kabuki world is related somehow, as either family or as *deshi* of the same teacher. In Japanese we refer to *deshi* of the same teacher as *kyodai deshi*, which means sibling *deshi*. In this way, living and working in the world of kabuki is like being in one large extended family.

In addition to the Narikoma-ya the important *onnagata yago* in Tokyo is Otowa-ya. Among *onnagata* this refers to the present Onoe Kikugoro VII and his father Onoe Baiko VII. In the twentieth century this is a line that was made famous by Kikugoro V

(1845–1903) who ranked with Danjuro IX as a leader of Meiji kabuki. His son Kikugoro VI (1885–1949) was responsible for many innovations in kabuki and is still so respected that he is referred to simply as *Rokudaime*, which means simply, "The Sixth."

Among Kansai actors there is also Kataoka Nizaemon who is the oldest actor still appearing on stage. As of this writing in 1988, he is eighty-five. His *yago* is Matsushima-ya. He comes from Kyoto and his second son is Kataoka Takao, an actor who has also achieved fame abroad acting with the popular young *onnagata* Bando Tamasaburo. Another actor whose roots ultimately are in Kansai is Nakamura Tomijuro V. His *yago* is Tennoji-ya which is named after the famous Tennoji temple in Osaka.

As a rule, an actor's oldest son succeeds to his name. If there are two sons, then as with Koshiro IX and Kichiemon II, the oldest son takes his father's name and the second son takes another name that doesn't have a holder at present. Since Koshiro succeeded his father while his younger brother succeeded his grandfather, from the standpoint of the family registry, we have the odd situation where, formally, a younger brother is his older brother's uncle.

The present Koshiro is the ninth of that name, his father was the eighth, and his mother was the daughter of the first Kichiemon. Kichiemon only had this one daughter, who married Koshiro and had two sons, Somegoro (the present Koshiro) and Kichiemon. Then the older brother succeeded his father and the younger brother succeeded his grandfather. It feels like the younger brother has gone and become a member of the older generation.

In other words, in addition to family names like Ichikawa, Kataoka and Matsumoto that are, of course, carried on from generation to generation, there are what we would regard as given names like Koshiro and Kichiemon which are also carried on without change from generation to generation. A new *deshi* usually receives the name of someone from the past; he can't just go and make up a new name on his own.

I received the name Nakamura Matazo II. Without receiving a proper name, one is not considered eligible to receive the traditions of performance. When I first became a *deshi* of Matagoro, there were many names available and I had a difficult time deciding what name I should take. Finally Matagoro suggested "Matazo," and that was that.

In order to succeed to an important name from another family, for the most part, the only way is through marriage. In other words, to be a true member of the group one has to have a real family tie. Many people have become the heads of traditions through marriage, often marriage to someone who is already distantly related.

If the marriage is not to another member of the kabuki world, it might be to a member of a *nagauta* music family or the head of a school of dance, in other words traditions that are closely associated with kabuki. It is extremely unusual for a kabuki actor to marry someone who is totally unrelated to the kabuki world. Kabuki tends to be a rather closed world which might be difficult for someone outside the kabuki world to understand and accept.

ATMOSPHERE

In the Edo period people used to go in and out of the auditorium during the play, and eat and drink as they watched. The atmosphere was more like that at a sumo wrestling tournament today. The audience members might drink and doze, but would wake up for the high points of the play. It was a challenge for an actor to attract and keep the audience's attention in such an atmosphere.

Today people sit through entire acts, and only eat and drink during the intermissions. As an actor, I would like to tell you to enjoy yourselves at the theater but not to make distracting noises which make it difficult for us to do our job.

Most members of the audience come in Western clothing, although of course there are more women in the audience wearing kimono than you usually see in public. This is partly because the audience tends to be traditional and likes traditional clothing, partly because many members of the audience are wealthy and can afford kimono, which are very expensive.

However, in the contrast between the actors on stage all wearing traditional clothing and the audience nearly all wearing Western clothing, we can see how distinct kabuki has become from the everyday world. The language on stage is also very different from modern Japanese, and young Japanese find it very difficult to understand. Unfortunately, not nearly enough is done in Japanese schools to introduce young people to traditional culture, and I find that even in Japan, my kabuki workshop serves a useful purpose in helping young people to understand kabuki.

The world of kabuki may seem distant from the world of the present, but as actors, our challenge is to bridge the time gap and to make the audience respond and be moved by the world of the Edo period, and in every performance we must face this challenge as if for the first time.

CHAPTER 7

Kabuki in the Classroom

One way of trying to identify what lies at the core of kabuki is to examine what kinds of things seem essential to mention whenever I talk about kabuki. Over the years I have had the good fortune to be involved with many different programs, both in Japan and abroad, which offer instruction in the elements of the many skills that a kabuki actor needs to master. This chapter describes some of our experiences in those programs.

In Chapter 2 I talked briefly about the National Theater's kabuki training program and its relationship to the traditional kabuki world. From the inception of this training program my teacher, Nakamura Matagoro, has been its chief instructor, and I have been fortunate enough to assist him in this important work. In its first eighteen years the program had forty-two graduates. Most of these young people are deeply attached to kabuki and have gone on to work in kabuki theater by becoming the *deshi* of an *onadai* actor. Some of them have, however, used their experience in training for a traditional performing art as the basis for other creative endeavors.

During the two-year program the students take part in several classes: acting, Japanese dance, Japanese stage fencing (*tachimawari*), tea ceremony, narrative reciting (*gidayu*), lyric singing accompanied by the *shamisen* (*nagauta*), and *taiko*. At the end of the first year the students are required to give a full-dress stage performance. This serves as an examination, and those who do not perform well are dismissed from the program. After another year of hard work those who continue are ready to become kabuki actors. Two years is really not enough time to master all of the basics, but we have trained many people who have become fine kabuki actors in this way.

The program accepts about ten people, both Japanese and foreign applicants, at a time. The most essential requirement is to have a flexible body that will be able to play many different roles. One of the characteristics of kabuki is the use of stylized expressions: an evil character, whatever his station in life or the nature of his particular villainy, will display certain expressions that communicate his wickedness; and so on for the whole range of characters that appear in kabuki dramas. Only a well-trained, disciplined body can create these stylized expressions convincingly.

Vocal training is also very important. The *gidayu* classes teach our students how to cultivate their voices, and how to master proper breathing The subtle pause is an important device in all Japanese traditional arts, and in kabuki it is effective only when breathing is controlled properly.

The old-style way to teach an actor or dancer is to have the student imitate the teacher until the action is perfected. This might also entail hitting the students, or knocking them over to impress on them physically the extent of their errors. Once, when scenes of Bando Yaenosuke—the late master of kabuki acrobatics—using these methods with the students of the National Theater training program were broadcast, there were complaints from the families of some of the students. Modern methods call for much more restraint on the teacher's part, but the student still has to learn to make the necessary motions effortlessly.

We have found that while the things we need to teach differ very little whether the student is a native Japanese or someone from abroad, some adjustments have to be made in specific techniques for our foreign students. Most of these derive not from cultural differences but from physical ones. For instance, in the seventeenth century when kabuki developed its now classic styles, the stature of the average Japanese was rather short, especially in the legs. So an actor had to open his legs out quite a long way to make a pose such as the *Genroku-mie* effective. The naturally long-legged student doesn't need to open his legs very wide at all to achieve the required effect; but he has to create a stance broad enough at the base to suggest a stable figure like a *butsuzo* (image of Buddha).

A similar kind of adjustment sometimes needs to be made in applying makeup. In particular, a man with a high-bridged nose looks apalling if he uses the same strong shadowing around his nose that most kabuki actors need.

Gesture is probably the main area in which there are differences that could be called cultural. When calling to someone, a Japanese will hold up his hand and flap it down with the palm facing outwards—this looks like "good-bye" to many Westerners, who call someone by holding the palm upwards and beckoning towards themselves. When indicating himself, a Japanese will point the forefinger at the tip of his nose. In the same situation a more typical Western gesture might be to point the thumb or four fingers at his breast. The same gesture can also have a different connotation in a different culture: when a Japanese makes a semi-circular gesture over his stomach, it means he has had enough to eat; to a Westerner this more often seems to be a way of indicating that someone else is pregnant or very fat.

There are also some points of historical background, not necessarily known by the Japanese students either, which affect in a general way certain kabuki practices. The most important of these is the custom maintained in Japanese traditional arts that the left side has higher priority than the right. This directional precedence is believed to have originated in China around 2000 B.C. It was introduced to Japan in the seventh century A.D. by Emperor Shotoku Taishi, who formally established the practice that the *Tenno* (Emperor) would sit in the middle, the *Sadaijin* (Minister of the Left) on the left, and the *Udaijin* (Minister of the Right) on the right. The Minister of the Left had the higher rank. In kabuki the tradition lives on in such practices as always taking the first step with the left leg.

Whoever our students are, we always find that there is one physical problem which has to be dealt with. Every traditional Japanese art requires the ability to be able to sit in the formal *seiza* kneeling position. Until not so very long ago this *seiza* position was part of daily Japanese life, the natural way to sit at the dinner table and in many other situations. This of course was in the days when nearly all homes had *tatami* mats and low-level tables. Now most homes are furnished with tables and chairs and fewer and fewer people, especially young people, can sit this way.

On the kabuki stage it is normal to have to sit in the *seiza* position for thirty or forty minutes. It is the same for noh and kyogen. So it is impossible to be an actor if you cannot do this. The first component of our training program is training in *seiza*, and people who cannot master this style of sitting usually quit within the first three months. Once you can get through fifteen minutes in this position, then increasing it to thirty minutes or more is not so difficult. That first fifteen minutes is the major hurdle. The problem is that most people, instead of sitting with the weight of the body balanced and resting lightly on the soles of their tucked-under feet, let their posterior slip toward the floor and end up resting their entire weight on their calves. This is why the legs go numb and sitting *seiza* becomes an excruciating experience.

There are times, however, when even experienced actors have problems with *seiza*. Some plays, like *Kanjincho* for example, call for some characters to sit on stage in the *seiza* position for almost their entire length. In *Kanjincho* Togashi Saemon, the official appointed to guard a barrier set to capture Yoshitune at Ataka, has three retainers with him. These three retainers do nothing but sit waiting behind their lord until he suddenly commands them to bring gifts to the traveling priests whom Togashi has decided to let through his post. One of my seniors once found that, after sitting like that for forty or forty-five minutes, one of his legs had gone numb so that when the command was given to bring out the gifts, he could not move. The other two retainers brought out their trays of rolls of silk and pouches of gold dust, but a *koken* assistant had to bring on the third one. That got the stricken actor through that part of the scene, but once the trays have been presented all three actors and supposed to make their exit. It is not at all easy, and it is also extremely painful, to have to try and inconspicuously massage a leg back into action without attracting the audience's attention, especially in a very short space of time. Although this actor did manage to make his exit, it is a good reminder of how important it is to master the *seiza* technique.

Minor characters do not move about the stage very much while a scene is in progress. They either perform their part and make their exit almost immediately, or else sit down quietly *seiza* style until the action is over. As a mark of respect, and to keep up our training, when a senior actor or one of the Living National Treasures who from time to time consent to give a lesson for the National Theater training program is giving a talk, all the students and the instructors sit *seiza* throughout the session.

KABUKI AND JAPANESE SCHOOLS

Another matter that often requires quite detailed attention is walking and posture. For someone who has never worn a kimono, it is difficult to appreciate that the way of walking and standing still is different from what you do in Western dress. Let me illustrate this with examples from two different special classes given in Japan.

Few young Japanese feel close to kabuki, or any of the traditional Japanese performing arts. The public school music curriculum is almost completely Western-music oriented, and any introduction to theater focuses on modern Western-style theater. Some young people, however, find their own way to appreciation of traditional arts through club activities at high school or college, and in some cases members of a kabuki club will learn about kabuki through training sessions in actual performance techniques. Since the 1950's I have worked with a number of such Kabuki Clubs, and at the moment am involved with two, very different, groups.

The first I will mention is at the Showa Music Conservatory, a school of Western music. When I was asked to help these students learn something of Japanese dance, I found it hard to imagine what the organizers were aiming for. But after watching a student performance of *Madame Butterfly*, I realized what their need was—the musical side of the performance was just fine, but none of the performers knew how to move in a kimono.

There is a scene set out in a garden which is spread with

gravel, and a stepping stone at the entrance of the house for people to stand on while removing their footwear before going inside. Pinkerton sits at a table and Madame Butterfly appears from the rear of the house bringing a tray of tea. She is dressed in a long kimono which trails behind her, but I was astonished to notice that she walks right out into the garden, without bothering to put on slippers or clogs, serves the tea and then goes straight back into the house without stopping to wipe her feet. Her maids do exactly the same—go out into the garden barefoot and walk straight back into the house. This would never be done in an ordinary Japanese home, whether in kimono or not. We always change our footwear at the entrance. This is especially important when wearing a elegant kimono whose hem is made to trail along the floor. The proper manner can be seen on the kabuki stage: whenever a female characters walks outside she either ties up the hem of her kimono to keep it from dragging on the ground, or, since this is after all on stage, she wears a brightly-colored sash to suggest that her hem has been tied up.

Whether the performers knew any of this is hard to say, but they certainly did not know how to move in a kimono. In one party scene a number of women move around, this time holding up their hems. The girls strode around as if they were wearing blue jeans, not with the legs kept together and modest steps that show kimono to its best advantage. We began our lessons with etiquette and deportment, postponing learning dance until the students could stand, sit, and walk, and generally wear kimono properly. It might make rather dry reading, but an outline of my lesson plan is included in the last chapter, and it gives a good idea of what points we focus on in early kabuki training sessions.

The situation was quite different with the second group, one at the girls' high school attached to Nihon Women's University. Again I was surprised, but for exactly the opposite reason. Every member of the club knew how to wear kimono and moved perfectly. These students all had an interest in classical arts— some of them were studying the tea ceremony, or were taking music lessons in the *koto* or the *shamisen*—and somehow they all possessed a polish that the other university students had not had. It is likely that it is not only those personal interests, but also other things in their background coming from their families and their school that gives these girls this accomplishment. Whatever the reason, it is encouraging to encounter a group of young people like this.

Many of the students from both of these groups, inspired by the classes or by seeing one of the annual performances put on specially for students under the sponsorship of the Ministry of Education, have gone to see full kabuki performance. Obviously they find something special in live kabuki that they cannot get from films or television. I suspect, however, that the enjoyment they derive from such experiences is based on an image of kabuki quite different from what I had in my youth. So much has changed from that time: these young people plan a trip overseas for summer vacation when they're still in high school; fifty years ago going abroad was a big event, and everyone worried whether the person would come back at all. My generation knew very little about the rest of the world; now it sometimes seems that today's young people know more about other countries than about the traditions of their own.

Some of the young people who have found ways of merging traditional arts with modern life are performers. Oida Yoshi began his career as an actor in the Bungaku-za, a well-known modern theater troupe. When he felt a need for further training and methods of expression, he took lessons as a *gidayu* narrative singer—he and I had the same teacher for *gidayu* and kyogen lessons. He already had some experience with the traditional *koto*, or thirteen-string Japanese harp, and he began to bring these skills in traditional media together to create performances that combined elements of Buddhism and Shinto in a narrative storytelling style.

At about this time the director of the Royal Shakespeare Company, Peter Brook, asked the Japanese Ministry of Education for help in identifying an actor with training in traditional performing arts who might be available to work with the company in England. Both Oida and I were approached, and he was the one free to go. In addition to the various traditional arts he had studied, he had over a decade of experience in modern Western drama with Bungaku-za, and he could speak English. He worked very successfully with Peter Brook's company for four or five years, and was one of the members who went to Africa on the "Conference of the Birds" tour, but he wanted to direct himself. He returned to Japan and formed his own troupe.

Recently Oida worked with Peter Brook again, and appeared in the 1988 performance in Japan of the epic Indian poem, *Mahabharata*.

There are also a number of overseas performers who have found something in kabuki that can be applied to their own art. In Europe, I have been surprised to learn, kabuki is considered avant-garde.

While teaching in West Berlin during an international theater festival sponsored by the International Theater Institute which featured many avant-garde plays, I attended one quite surrealistic performance. The stage was just a square space marked off on the floor by ropes, like a boxing ring. There was no set, except for some ropes suspended from the ceiling at the "corners" of this "room." The audience sat on the floor around this space and the actors came on from either side and presented a play, a work by the German avant-garde playwright Heiner Muller. The script was a selection of texts from Ibsen and a variety of Russian and Polish writers, and the music was all sound effects. Without my interpeter I would never have known what the story was about.

It was these avant-garde artists who told me how they were attracted to kabuki because of the way it transcended the boundaries of time and space. It surprised me that they found this attractive and interesting, because it is exactly this aspect which young Japanese audiences find difficult to understand. For example, in the kyogen interlude of the kabuki dance, *Renjishi*, the actor has the line: "That is certainly a magnificent mountain. In the time that it takes to say that I see that I have already arrived in the capital." He says this as he circles the stage, and in this simple way represents his journey from Osaka to Kyoto in an instant. This is a very old technique, deriving from classic noh and kyogen. The young German performers found it fresh and new, and were fascinated by this way of representing the passage of great distance and time in a matter of seconds.

Some Western theater artists have come to Japan to study aspects of kabuki. Among them are two European women whose interest is in choreography. One is a Dutch ballet teacher, and the other a German dancer who combined lessons in kabuki dance with study with Ohno Kazuo, a pioneer in the rather brutal avant-garde dance form called butoh.

We used the play *Musume Dojoji*, which takes the noh tale of a woman turned into a serpent by her jealous fury who destroys the bell of the Dojoji Temple to take revenge on the priest who had rejected her advance. It starts with the dedication ceremony for a new bell to replace the one destroyed earlier. Although the head priest has declared that no women are to be allowed in the temple grounds on this important day, a court dancer appears and talks the priests into permitting her to perform a dance in celebration of this new bell. Her dance magically lulls the priests to sleep, and then she attacks the bell. This dancer is, of course, the spirit of the woman, which has returned to destroy once again the symbol of her unattainable love.

Both women were inspired by the story to create their own versions of *Dojoji*, and I was surprised and intrigued by the results. The German dancer created a butoh version of *Musume Dojoji* and performed it in a small studio space. On the left side of the studio there were two television monitors, two more on the right and one in the center; five monitors in all. To the sound of contemporary music, she made her entrance. Her costume was quite different from the red kimono and gold court cap used in kabuki; she entered wearing a long, sheer wine-colored dress. The only point her performance had in common with the kabuki play was that it also treated a woman driven mad by disappointment in love, but still I was very interested by the experiment.

The ballet dancer's version of *Musume Dojoji* used a tower about two meters high made of iron pipes. She dangled from this tower, climbed on top of it, and lay down on her side on it. It was as though she had adapted some of the acrobatic stage tricks of kabuki—which are not used in *Musume Dojoji*—for her dance. She used the rhythmical sounds of Japanese *taiko* drums to accompany her movements. Both of these artists were inspired by some element of kabuki, enriching their own creations.

Also, many directors have been inspired by Japanese theater. I have already mentioned Peter Brook's interest, but there are other top directors who are attracted to kabuki and other forms of Japanese theater. By gathering together actors from different backgrounds something new is bound to appear, and the skills of Japanese traditional performers are a part of this mixture.

In her production of Shakespeare's *Richard II*, French director Ariane Mnouchkine used a *hanamichi* runway, had stage assistants appear dressed all in black, and used kabuki-style costumes. From beginning to end the play was accompanied by the pulsing sound of Japanese *taiko* drums. There were backdrops painted with the setting and the scenes were changed by having the backdrops fall to the ground one by one to reveal the dozen or so scenes in turn. Clearly this technique was inspired by the kabuki *asagi* curtain which is the light blue curtain that conceals the stage at the beginning of a scene and drops to reveal the setting.

Robert Wilson is another artist who has been inspired by Japan. In 1983 he came to Japan for a workshop for the Japanese portion of *The Civil WarS*—the epic theater piece created for the Los Angeles Olympic Games. *The Civil WarS* was assembled separately all over the world, and the Japanese workshop was held for one day in the Hanae Mori building. He brought together a very unusual group of Japanese performers, including noh actors, kyogen actors, kabuki actors, members of Suzuki Tadashi's company, and the butoh dance group, Sankai Juku.

Kanze Hideo was the representative for noh-style acting techniques and I represented kabuki acting techniques. When Wilson first started directing us we were very puzzled. He asked us to perform noh or kabuki movements, but we never think of what we are doing in that way, we are always performing something. Finally, I decided to do Tomomori's dance from *Funa Benkei* and Kanze Hideo also selected a piece. Wilson worked to combine and compose what he saw in his own way.

Unfortunately, *The Civil WarS* was never performed in its entirety, due to lack of funds, but the results of the various workshops have been performed, usually with great success.

These are some of the artists that I have seen who have been influenced by kabuki and other forms of Japanese theater. I hope that in the future there will be more understanding of kabuki and more interesting experiments.

For over ten years I have been involved with introducing kabuki around the world, and one thing that constantly surprises me is the response of Japanese abroad. Very often they will come to performances out of a sense of duty and then be so thrilled by the performance that they come up to us later and say, "I never knew that kabuki was so *interesting!*" In Japan and abroad there is still much to be done to communicate this message.

EARLY ADVENTURES TEACHING ABROAD

One of our earliest successes in giving a course on kabuki acting was in 1978 when the theater department of the University of Hawaii invited Nakamura Matagoro, Nakamura Shijaku and myself to train a group of students for a performance of *Chushingura*.

Books on Japan were, of course, very popular among the students of Japanese there, and nearly all the sixty students in the classes that we taught had read the English translations of Suzuki Daisetsu's books on Zen and Mishima Yukio's *Five Modern Noh Plays*. Apparently this was the image American college students had of Japan at the time. Some students, perhaps looking for something more sophisticated, had also read Edward Seidensticker's translation of *The Tale of Genji*. Interesting as these books are, modern Japan really isn't a combination of Zen, Mishima and elegant courtly romance from the twelfth century. I don't know how much these books helped the students to understand a tale of samurai loyalty like *Chushingura*, but I do believe that more and more people have come to feel that in order to understand Japan it is important to study the Edo period. The most creative form of theater during the Edo period was kabuki, so that if one is studying the performing arts of Japan, kabuki should be considered as at least as important as noh.

The University of Hawaii had a rather international feeling which reminded me of my own days as a college student at Sophia University in the 1950s.

There has been a long tradition of kabuki at the University of

Hawaii, and much effort is put into continuing that tradition. The head of the theater department has lived in Japan, knows Japanese, and is of course familiar with live kabuki. At the University of Hawaii he worked with the students to try and reproduce kabuki plays authentically, although the texts were translated into English. But after seeing so much live kabuki, he knew that his student actors needed help with more than the text to produce a play like the kabuki original. In order to do that special training was needed, and so he raised the funds to have my teacher, Matagoro, and two assistants go and spend six months trying to train a group of American students to re-create *Chushingura*.

When we got there, we found about sixty students divided in-to two classes. There was one class of general students who were studying kabuki as an elective. The other group was majoring in kabuki and had much greater demands—the members of this group were scheduled to give public performances of *Chushingura* in six months. Kabuki always depends on music, so we also arranged a music class. We were lucky enough to find a fine teacher, Yamada Chie, already at the university, and she taught the students *gidayu* music, the narrative music from the bunraku puppet theater that is used in *Chushingura*, and *geza ongaku*, the background music of kabuki. The students would be unable to perform unless they could understand the words of the *gidayu* narrator well enough to coordinate their actions with the narration, and unless they understood the meaning and rhythm of the different pieces of background music, they would be unable to coordinate their movements with the music well enough to communicate its meaning to the audience.

Our first task was to have the kabuki majors sit on the floor in *seiza* formal kneeling position from nine in the morning until noon. When we arrived the first morning, the students had already assembled. Three or four of the women in the class were wearing cotton *yukata* and sitting *seiza* on the floor. We were im-pressed that these students in *yukata* were so well prepared. It turned out that in order to prepare for the kabuki performance, some months before that these women had started studying Japanese dance outside of class. Aside from these women, most of the other students were wearing all kinds of rehearsal clothes.

Although in Honolulu it would not be that difficult for the students to get *yukata* or kimono, we decided to leave the choice of rehearsal clothing up to the students.

The lessons began with how to bow sitting on the floor. You have to put your hands in front of you and then bow, but many students bent their heads down too far, looking very servile. When bowing properly in the Japanese fashion, it is necessary to hold one's back and head out straight, and to bow from the waist. It is necessary to exert a lot of strength from the waist, and we learned that this is a very difficult thing for people who have spent their lives sitting in chairs.

I later heard a story about an American dancer who unknowingly made use of these motions that most Americans are unaccustomed to. The dancer, Alvin Ailey, was in an automobile accident and for some time after he was unable to move. During that time, he thought up exercises that he could do in bed and was later a great success when he used these movements in his jazz dance.

In kabuki there are movements that are used in the stage fights called *tachimawari*. One movement is called *miso suri*, a term that describes bean paste being ground with a mortar and pestle. In this movement, the performer gets into a crawling position. With both hands on the floor, the weight of the body balances on one knee while the other leg is extended, and the performer pushes his body around so it whirls and one leg is moving in a circle like the hand of a clock. Movements like this are certainly bed exercises. The term can also be used to describe other movements from kneeling positions like opening and closing *fusuma* sliding screens or *shoji* paper-covered screens, which are moved in a half-crouching position called *kiza*.

The rules of etiquette which prescribe this position for opening and closing screens come from rules of behavior for samurai. The rules are not just empty ceremony but emphasize order and stable body positions that also produce the constant alertness and capacity for instant movement that a samurai would need in the event of a sudden attack.

In the Japanese traditional performing arts it is considered beautiful to keep the body's center of gravity low so that all the movements are very stable. Western ballet is the opposite; when one walks, one moves dynamically, with the upper body reaching out for the sky. When walking this way there is of course a certain amount of strength coming from the hip muscles, but this is different from the kabuki technique called *koshi o ireru*. My wife is a classical ballet teacher with thirty years of experience, and she also studied Japanese dance when she was a child so that she can compare *koshi o ireru* in ballet and Japanese dance. She tells me that it is quite different from "contraction," as it is called in ballet. When you walk in ballet, you keep your stomach in, and the muscles of the hips and buttocks firm. In Japanese dance the stomach sticks out since one bends slightly at the waist and keeps the stomach in front of the hips, then walks with knees slightly bent.

This way of walking with knees bent seemed very unnatural to the students at the University of Hawaii who had had ballet experience, but for that very reason they found it interesting. In noh and kabuki, this position of *koshi o ireru* allows an actor to keep a position with the upper body absolutely stable while his balance is maintained with the lower body. This is an appropriate position for the art form of an agricultural people: when wearing heavy clogs in a muddy rice field, standing with one's weight low, the only way to walk is with the sliding *suri ashi* step.

ROLE PLAYING

Unlike ballet, we never learn kabuki movement as pure form, but as acting. For example, when we practice *suri ashi*, instead of learning the walk first and adding characterization later, from the very beginning we learn to walk in the style of a particular role—from the arrogant poised walk of nobles and samurai on the one hand to the humble shuffle of farmers and townspeople on the other. Then, for female roles, we also practice the different ways of walking for nobility and women serving in samurai houses—women used to elegance and authority—and farming and urban women—women used to manual labor—on the other. For any role, an *onnagata*, or man playing a female role, must walk with much smaller steps than its male counterpart. There are other refinements as well. A geisha walks alluringly, waving her shoulders and sticking out her chest. And for very high-ranking courtesans there is a special walking technique called *hachi monji* or "figure eight" where she slowly drags the inside edge of very high clogs in a graceful circle with each step, a reminder of the days when courtesans would parade through the pleasure quarters with a large crowd of attendants.

Even though *Chushingura* focuses on samurai, in the course of a full-length performance a whole host of characters appears. Samurai of all ranks, from the brother of the shogun to lowly footsoldiers, farmers, merchants, and courtesans. We had to train our actors to express all these different types of people physically, through movement, rather than through the more familiar psychological approach of the realistic theater.

The problem was that the time was too short to train the actors in all these movements until they became second nature. But even if the time was too short, it was also very important to treat these students just as seriously as we treated our students at the National Theater. If teachers are less than one hundred percent serious about what they teach, the students will come to take a half-formed, imperfect art as their standard.

Some cultural differences, particularly in gesture, made it difficult for the students to appreciate the significance of many movements and they thought them just empty style, although they were movements that seem quite mundane to us, even if rather exaggerated and stylized.

In the bombastic style of kabuki called *aragoto*, a character usually gestures with his fingers splayed out and the entire hand held so that palm and fingers form a flat plane. Even ordinary gestures such as beckoning and pointing are performed with these exaggerated hand positions. But *onnagata* always keep their fingers together with the thumb tucked under in order to make the hand look as small and delicate as possible. This is helped by keeping the hands just at the opening of the kimono sleeve, and to do this, the actor keeps his elbows against his body. An *onnagata* performs the same gestures with small, graceful movements. These conventions mean that an *onnagata* can never do something like folding his arms on stage.

Through careful teaching of the gestures appropriate to each role type, we gradually moved from basic exercises to the movements that the students would use in the actual play.

A kabuki actor begins his physical training with learning to distinguish among the movements specific to different role types. There seems to be a lot of resistance to role types among actors who have been trained for the realistic stage where individual characterization is more important than role types. But for a kabuki actor, the road to individuality begins in copying his teacher exactly. If mannerisms are not eliminated first and an individual style is encouraged from the beginning, the result will be to arrest an actor's progress. It is extremely difficult to separate mannerisms from individualism, which is why it is important in the beginning stages to encourage and awaken a sense of receptivity in the actor so that he can imitate his teacher as closely as possible. Anyone can walk, but a truly beautiful walk free of mannerisms is surprisingly difficult to achieve. It is said that ten years of basic training is needed for kabuki. At the University of Hawaii we had nothing like that kind of time. We had to give both concentrated training in kabuki and teach *Chushingura* in the space of six months. Even so, for the first month we didn't look at the text of *Chushingura*. We spent that first month going through the fundamentals of movement. In the second month we finally began the lines and actions of *Chushingura* from the prologue. By this time the head of the department had finished the translating and adapting of the script.

There were some difficulties in translating the play, and from time to time he consulted us on how to read difficult names, and other problem spots. For example, there was the word *funa samurai*, which literally means "carp-samurai." This is a term that the villain uses to insult the hero of the play. Both *funa* and *koi* are translated as "carp" in English, but in Japanese the two varieties of carp have very different associations. *Koi* is considered an auspicious fish and in Japan you can see ponds full of black and red *koi* as a sign of good fortune. *Funa*, on the other hand, conjures up images of something raised in a dirty, muddy place so that it suggests someone uncouth, a fish that comes from a spot far from civilization. It was not easy to communicate the implications of an unsophisticated samurai from the country with the fish image. So someone suggested "tadpole" instead, to imply a samurai who is not yet fully grown.

Names are a problem too because some names are words with meaning that give clues to the characters and some are not names at all but titles that change depending on who is speaking to whom. As a rule, we finally decided to stick with Japanese versions of proper names. There were many translation problems like this, but to discuss them all would take too long and not really help explain how to deliver lines in kabuki.

Just as every role type has a particular way of walking, it also has a particular way of talking. When an actor creates an individual character, it is by using elements of these role types. In Hawaii, we had the difficult task of training the students to deliver lines in English in the vocal styles developed for the Japanese language. In some cases this worked and in others it didn't. But though we would have liked to have more time to teach the students perfectly, even as much as they could learn was often very effective. The lines are part of a larger picture where staging is more important than the text.

In most Western drama, including Shakespeare, it is considered normal for the lines of a play to have a kind of logical, narrative progression. In kabuki there are many cases where atmosphere and emotion are more important than logic. When there are moments where the lines are a little odd from a logical point of view, usually the effect is carried by music or colorful staging.

Sometimes, even in an historical play, the costuming has nothing to do with the historical period it is supposed to be depicting. *Chushingura* is a good example of this. Although the incident it is based on took place in December 1701, it is set in the Kamakura period in the twelfth century and the names of all involved are changed.

The costumes are colorful and spectacular approximations of eighteenth-century samurai dress. In the opening prologue known as the *dai jo* (great prologue), the three main characters wear costumes in strikingly contrasting colors to set them apart. One character is all in black, another in light blue, another yellow. For this reason we can tell at a glance the difference between the villain, Moronao, who is in black, the first victim of his rage, the young hot-headed Wakasanosuke, who is in light blue, and the gentle Enya Hangan, in yellow, who is the eventual victim of the tragedy and whose retainers avenge him by killing Moronao. The selection of colors for the major actor and the visual spectacle carries the drama more than the text.

In our six months in Hawaii, Matagoro taught all the details of production that he could. The basic training also paid off since it meant that people could move properly in their costumes, expressing the role types of their characters and looking neat and beautiful at the same time. This combination of beauty and expressive drama is the heart of kabuki. The head of the department paid special attention to all these important points of production in order to put on a splendid *Chushingura*. It was performed with great success at the University of Hawaii, and then went on to tour, visiting universities across the United States and introducing American college students to what could be achieved with hard work and the proper training and showing them the traditional art of kabuki in a form easier to feel at home with than kabuki in Japanese.

CHAPTER **8**

Kabuki Workshop

In an earlier chapter I discussed the kind of instruction that is given in the National Theater's training program for kabuki actors. The approach described in this chapter is that used in a rather different situation—a kabuki workshop for foreigners. A Japanese person who knows nothing at all about kabuki still has an intuitive understanding for much of its content because it is part of his cultural heritage. In the workshop we complement specialized kabuki instruction with explanations of points on cultural background.

To give you an idea of what you would experience in such a workshop, I will describe a typical demonstration using excerpts from the dance-drama *Funa Benkei* (Benkei in the Boat). It is quite a recent play, adapted for the kabuki stage from a noh play in 1885, but it is perfect for demonstrating several aspects of kabuki, especially since the main character in the first half of the play is a woman, and in the second half a male ghost.

Without any preliminary introduction, the curtain opens and I appear as a court dancer. Dressed simply in a red kimono with a noh-style gold fan, I circle the stage making graceful gestures with the fan, ending the dance in tears. The woman's grief is indicated simply by a hand held in front of her face to hide her tears. This simple and eloquent gesture originates in noh.

After this excerpt I take off the costume and makeup and return to explain the play. Whenever possible I like to begin dancing without explanation, so that the members of the audience have an opportunity to react directly to the art form itself. Afterwards, they have something to refer to as various aspects of kabuki are explained.

Funa Benkei is about a general named Yoshitsune. His brother, Yoritomo, is shogun, and has been tricked into believing that his brother is a traitor and is trying to have him killed. Yoshitsune takes flight from his brother's forces, and relies on the strength and wisdom of his companion Benkei. Another part of this journey is the subject of the play *Kanjincho*, but here the subject is Yoshitsune's departure by boat.

Yoshitsune's lover, a woman who is a court dancer or *shirabyoshi* named Shizuka Gozen follows, hoping to go along, but Benkei is forced to say that they cannot take a woman along on this desperate journey. After performing a sad dance, Shizuka Gozen parts from Yoshitsune forever. The demonstration dance is a section of Shizuka Gozen's dance.

While the story of *Funa Benkei* is being told, some assistants bring out a little table, with a mirror and makeup on it, and set it center stage. As they bring out my costume for the second half of *Funa Benkei* and set it on the stage to one side of the table, I explain the second half of *Funa Benkei*.

One advantage of using a play that originates in noh is that in noh there is only one principal actor at a time, an actor called the *shite*. This means that a single performer can convey the essence of the play without a large crowd of supporting actors. The character that the *shite* plays in the first half is Shizuka Gozen, and the audience can see for itself how, among other things, an actor takes tiny steps and conceals his hands within the sleeves of his kimono to make them look smaller, in order to create the impression that he is a woman.

In the second half of the play, Yoshitsune and his companions set out by boat but suddenly a storm blows up and a figure brandishing a halberd appears walking on the rough waves. It is the ghost of Tomomori, one of the many warriors killed in the sea battle with Yoshitsune's forces. He has come to drag Yoshitsune down into the sea, but Benkei, who is a *yamabushi* or mountain priest, fends the ghost off with prayers and his rosary, allowing Yoshitsune to escape safely.

In the second half of the demonstration, I will perform a section of the dramatic dance that the ghost of Tomomori performs, threatening Yoshitsune with his halberd until Benkei finally vanquishes the ghost. In the noh theater Tomomori is the main character, and Yoshitsune and Benkei have supporting roles. During the workshop demonstration the audience has to imagine what they are doing from Tomomori's actions.

Tomomori is played in the style called *aragoto*, and his face is made up with bold *kumadori* lines drawn in blue. Sitting at the table, I begin applying my makeup for the Tomomori role and as I do this I talk generally about kabuki make-up. There is no fixed script for this commentary, and the amount of detail given depends on the reason for the workshop and the amount of time available. Appropriate portions of the following information is given.

Makeup

Kabuki employs a wide variety of makeup styles, from the stylized *kumadori* makeup with colored lines on a white base, to the pure white faces of female characters with red highlights at the eyes and delicate pink shading, to relatively naturalistic flesh colors for ordinary merchants and farmers. Nearly all kabuki makeup is waterbase, not greasepaint. *Dohran* (the Japanese word for grease paint, derived from the German) and pancake are widely used in other forms of theater, but centuries of experience have shown that water-based makeup produces the best colors for kabuki. Also, in other forms of theater there may be professionals who apply the makeup, but in kabuki each actor puts on his own makeup, and he takes great pride in his skill in drawing the expressive lines that create a powerful *kumadori* design, or the subtle touches that create an alluring female face.

Most makeup begins with the white base called *oshiroi*. It is extremely difficult to give the face the flawless white color kabuki demands. Like all water-based makeup, *oshiroi* must be carefully applied because if wet makeup is applied over dry makeup, the shades of white will not match.

Records show that during the Nara period (eighth century), white face makeup or *oshiroi* was prepared from chestnuts or glutinous rice. At the same time *oshiroi* made with lead was also imported from China. Because lead is poisonous, today most *oshiroi* is synthetic. To apply kabuki's water-based makeup, we use a brush called an *ita-hake* (board brush), which is a few inches wide but only a fraction of an inch thick, like a thin board.

First I paint my neck with the *ita-hake*, and then even the *oshiroi* out with a small block of sponge. This allows the skin to soak up the coloring. Then, with whatever whitener is left in the sponge, I just whiten my nose. Taking up the *ita-hake* again, I paint my entire face white, and dab it with the sponge. For some reason, actors from Kyoto and Osaka, in the Kansai region, do it in the opposite order. First they paint their face and then their necks.

There is a convention that roles played with white skin are starring roles, while roles played with brown faces are supporting roles. This is probably because people of low social status who worked outdoors had tanned skin, unlike people of high social status who stayed indoors and prized fine pale skin. Another convention is to show villains with red faces. This probably shows not only that their social status is low, but that they are heavy drinkers, with big red noses.

Some roles call for *kumadori* makeup with red, blue or brown lines painted on the white base. Each of these colors has a meaning. Red expresses strength, blue indicates that the character is not human, but a ghost. Brown shows that the character is some kind of creature, as in the role of the spirit of the earth spider in *Tsuchi Gumo*, which uses brown face makeup and *kumadori* lines in a darker color over that. For most of these roles, makeup is applied not only to the face, but to any other parts of the body that show. On occasion, *kumadori* lines are painted on other parts of the body as well, for example, strong red lines on an *aragoto* hero's arms and legs. On these occasions, *kumadori* lines are drawn on to a kind of body stocking.

The conventions are different from those of the Chinese Peking Opera. There it is not heroes but villains who have their faces painted white. Things are also different in the European comic tradition, where clowns, or Pierrot, appear in whiteface. Depending on the country, the meaning of a white face can change this much. I wonder what significance people in other countries attach to roles played with a red face.

During the Edo period, society was divided into four classes: samurai, farmer, craftsman, and merchant, with the samurai at the top. Samurai swaggered about, carrying the two swords that were the badges of their power and prestige. The lowly merchants were forbidden to carry anything more than a short blade, but were much better off financially than the samurai who, as a class, viewed commerce with disdain. To a samurai of the Genroku period, genteel poverty was noble, as reflected in a saying of the times: "Even when he was starving, a samurai used a fine toothpick." Yet it distressed them to see the low-ranking merchants leading lives of economic plenty. The samurai resented these upstarts to the extent that they would bully the commoners on the slightest pretext, and from time to time would draw their swords and kill commoners without being punished for it. After three hundred years of peace, no matter how much the samurai prided themselves on being warriors they did not keep up their martial arts skills, but even if one samurai alone was not much of a threat, a large group of samurai could easily bully a single merchant.

During this period, in the second half of the seventeenth century, an actor named Ichikawa Danjuro became popular in Edo. It was this great actor, the founder of the long Ichikawa line, who created the bombastic style of acting called *aragoto*. His appearance on the kabuki stage bellowing *Shibaraku!* (Wait a minute!) provided the people of Edo with a hero to come and cut down troublesome samurai. The superman role of Kamakura Gongoro was that of a samurai, but he was clearly a savior for the commoners who, after years of being insulted and despised must have given their overwhelming approval to this vindication of the many injustices perpetrated against them by the samurai. If this superman had appeared in the guise of a commoner the authorities would undoubtedly have banned the production. The *kumadori* makeup technique is an important element in the *aragoto* style of acting which enables kabuki actors to project the personality of their role so powerfully.

At the National Theater Kabuki Training Program, as a form of physical training in the fundamental points of movement, we always teach *Kurumabiki* (The Carriage Fight) as a representative *aragoto* play. The scene is often thought of as a part of the puppet play *Sugawara Denju Tenarai Kagami*, for which a number of English translations are available. Originally,

Matazo applies the *kumadori*
makeup for the role of Tomomori
in *Funa Benkei* during his workshop. The dark lines are black and
the lighter are blue. Note the importance of shading. Photo by
Morita Toshiro.

however, *Kuruma Biki* was an *aragoto* routine that had nothing
to do with the story of *Sugawara no Michizane*. It was inserted into kabuki adaptations of the puppet play, and then, unusually,
taken back in the opposite direction for new productions of the
puppet play.

The three protagonists, brothers with conflicting loyalties, are
young men of great physical strength and are played with white
faces and red *kumadori* makeup. One of them carries three
swords, instead of the normal two swords of a samurai, and is required to shout his lines. These swords are much larger than normal—the largest is two meters long—yet the part calls on him to
run the length of the *hanamichi*. The part requires great
physical strength and endurance, and it is the actor's victory
over his own physical limitations that enables him to depict a
character of superhuman strength.

I like to equate this process with a coming-of-age ritual.
Throughout the world young people are called on to pass some
test of endurance or strength in their passage to adulthood, and
in the kabuki world the training for *aragoto* roles can be such a
test. An actor must not only train his muscles, but learn to coordinate his movements with the vocal and breathing control
needed to deliver his lines. It is often said that for kabuki actors

voice comes first, then movement, and then figure and bearing. An actor must train his voice. How he looks can come later.

There is an interesting term in kabuki using the word *kesho*, or makeup. It is *kesho goe*, which means, literally, cosmetic voice. While a star is busy acting at the front of the stage, a large crowd stands at the back of the stage and chants *Arya! Korya!* to build up excitement. In other words, the term refers to a chant that adorns the acting of the star.

WIGS

Next I might show the audiences some different styles of wig. The female styles look very complicated. In the Edo period most women wore their hair pulled back from the forehead, with some sort of light support for the sidelocks so that they framed the upper half of the face with a graceful inverted U-shape. The front and sidelocks were tied to the top of the head. Then the back hair, which was allowed to grow long, was gathered, leaving a fall of hair around the neck, and then tied to the top of the head. The remaining length of hair at the back was then spread out into a bun, or perhaps gathered and folded. Of course, hairstyles varied with period and class. Some ages fancied very round sidelocks and top bun, others preferred sleeker styles with the sidelocks pulled in much closer for a slimmer, more elegant look. Yet other periods saw the hair let down at the back, with a comb put in rakishly on the side for a more provocative look.

Probably the most fantastic kabuki creations are the wigs for high-ranking courtesans. The sidelocks are brought out very far, and the topknot is pulled out into a large flat circle which looks almost like a halo. Luxurious combs of boxwood and tortoise shell decorate the hair along with large decorative hairpins, which might also be of tortoise shell. In the elegant parlors of Edo-period brothels, such courtesans must have been a stunning sight, as all their ornaments caught and reflected the flickering candlelight.

Women who served at the Imperial court and in Shinto shrines wore their hair long and drawn together at the back. This is also the style used for wigs in the noh theater, and the wig used in Shizuka's dance is of this type.

Men of the samurai class shaved the top of their heads, a custom originating in the days of constant warfare. Since a full head of hair was very hot and uncomfortable under the helmet of a suit of armor, the warriors shaved the top of their heads to let air flow in under the helmet. Then they gathered the remaining hair into a topknot, or *mage* (from the word *mageru*, meaning "to bend"), which was bent forward to provide a place for the helmet to rest. Even though warfare was only a memory in the Edo period, the style continued as a mark of the samurai class. A samurai boy had the top of his head shaved, but retained his forelock until it was shaved off as a sign of having attained adulthood. Many commoners also shaved their heads.

There are two basic types of male hairstyle, those with the hair cut short in back, which are usually samurai styles, and with the hair left long so that the back hair can be gathered and tied to the top of the head leaving a graceful fall of hair in back like the female styles. The hair from the back, sidelocks, and front was tied to the top of the head and the remaining length of hair gathered and pulled straight and then folded over so that it lay on the pate pointing forward. Women's hair styles may seem much more complicated, but in fact there are many more male styles with subtle differences in shape and proportion to fit the finest distinctions of class, office and occupation.

Of course, not all kabuki wig styles had real-life equivalents. The wigs of *aragoto* characters are pure fantasy. For example, there is one with sidelocks called *kuruma bin*, or "carriage sidelocks" because the sidelocks are rods of hair hardened with the waxy grease used to dress hair. The rods stick out from the side of the head like carriage spokes. Another imaginary hair style is the full mane-like wig that is used for ghosts, non-human characters and powerful villains. One of these styles is similar to a kind of wig used in noh, and is the wig worn as the ghost of Tomomori.

Wigs are made of hair that is attached to metal skullcaps. When a wig is made, the wigmaker begins by taking curved pieces of metal and then rivets them together to fit an individual actor's head perfectly. The hair is then attached to this base and styled.

The wigs are made by one set of craftsmen and dressed by

another set. The wigmaker's job ends when the wig reaches the theater. The wig dresser or *tokoyama* must be there every day to put the wigs on the actors and to keep them clean and in good shape. As with real hair, this means that with many styles every few days they must redo the hairstyle completely.

In the Edo period, of course, actors often wore their hair in the styles that they used on stage. But just as often the styles were different, especially for *onnagata*, so that wigs were used. However, if an actor had full sidelocks ballooning on the side of his head, or perhaps a fancy full topknot above, there would be no room for a wig on top of that. While in the theater, actors wore their hair in a style called *yakusha mage* or "actor's topknot" which was a style with sidelocks close to the head and a low unobtrusive topknot which allowed an actor to wear hairpieces to suit his part as he changed from one role to another.

THE HABUTAE

In modern kabuki, before applying his makeup, an actor puts a cloth cap called a *habutae* on his head. Putting on this piece of silk is an integral part of the kabuki makeup ritual. During the Edo period actors redid their hair every day so that it would fit under a wig. The idea of concealing one's own hair with the *habutae* cloth originated at the end of the Edo period and was thought up by a female *deshi* of Ichikawa Danjuro IX (1838–1903). Since women had been banned from the kabuki stage since 1629, this female kabuki actor—who was named Kumehachi—was a great exception indeed.

At the time, Japanese women wore their hair extremely long. It is said that Kumehachi came up with the idea of using a cloth cap because with long hair it was impossible to play male roles. With the *habutae* it was possible to dress one's hair to play a variety of roles. Also, when painted, the *habutae* cloth cap made an actor's face look bigger. At the time, theaters were only illuminated with oil lamps and candles so that it was necessary to try to make an actor stand out as much as possible in the dim light.

Apart from the highly exaggerated *aragoto* acting style, much kabuki acting is relatively naturalistic. There are many plays dealing with the events of daily life, a style of play especially

associated with Kyoto and Osaka. When Chikamatsu Monzaemon's play *Sonezaki Shinju* (The Love Suicide at Sonezaki)
is produced, the acting is very realistic. In many ways it is quite
similar to a period drama on television.

One difference, however, stands out between period dramas
on television and kabuki productions. Although the image per-
sists in many foreign countries that Japanese dramas on stage
and television deal mainly with kimono-clad characters, it is now
far more common, on stage as in everyday life, for Japanese to
wear Western-style clothes. As a result, when a play does call for
a character to wear kimono, actors still tend to move in the same
way as they would in Western dress. Modern productions reveal
the same inability to realistically present aspects of the traditional way of life in many other areas, for instance in the
delivery of lines. Much of kabuki, however, directly reflects the
old way of life of the samurai, and so preserves a far greater
realism in its customs.

A good example is in the use of the *habutae*. Recently it seems
that television actors playing the part of eighteenth-century
samurai know nothing about putting on the kabuki *habutae*.
This is most unfortunate, because it could be just as effective a
makeup technique on television as in kabuki, even though the
details of the process are much more difficult than it might
seem. When an actor plays a male role, often the top of his head
is painted blue. This is done by painting the *habutae* cap blue—
it stays exposed since the wig has only the topknot and
sidelocks. Between the top of the head and the forehead the
color changes to skin color. Blue is used because it suggests the
color of a shaved scalp, and mixing just the right shade of blue
for this purpose is extremely difficult.

The shaved pate is called the *sakayaki*, and in kabuki its color
in period plays and domestic plays is subtly different. In the
more stylized period plays the *sakayaki* is painted a pure blue; in
the more realistic domestic plays a little brown and black is mixed in to produce a slightly different color. In films and television
different colors again are used. It is extremely difficult to get
just the right color for the occasion. The best way for a kabuki actor to learn to mix these different colors is to ask his elders for instruction and watch carefully. This is not a technique allowing

for expression of individuality. The color appropriate to a role in a period play is fixed, as is the standard color used for the *sakayaki* in domestic kabuki.

After putting on his *habutae* and makeup an actor puts on his costume. Then he puts on his wig, and last of all paints his arms and hands. This is done last so that the white makeup does not come off onto the wig as it is pulled on. *Oshiroi* makeup is very difficult to remove from a wig, and the wig makers are very unhappy with any actor who gets makeup on one—there is an unexpectedly simple rationale for some of the ways of kabuki.

There is a wig called *hyaku nichi katsura* (hundred-day wig). This is worn by a character who has been unable to visit the barber and have his *sakayaki* properly shaved for a long time, so that the hair on the top of his head has all grown out. This wig is often used for thieves. On the other hand there is a wig used for romantic leads that has its pate properly shaved and is very light around the sides and the back. It is not just the state of the hair and the way it is dressed that is symbolic. Hair can also make a wider reference to a fundamental difference in type.

In the play *Tsuchi Gumo* (The Earth Spider), the spirit of the earth spider, which is a role played wearing a wig with a large shock of hair, may be seen to represent the native people, while the smooth-skinned warriors that vanquish it become the ruling class of the land it had dominated. A similar example of hirsuteness is found in the play *Suzu ga Mori* which was named after the site of an execution ground. A large crowd of thieves appears, their villainy implied in their being hairy all over, an effect that is achieved by wearing body stockings with the hair painted on.

The wig that is worn in the role of the ghost of Taira no Tomomori, which people attending the workshop will see in the second half of the demonstration, is a large one with masses of hair. Does this mean that the role is one of a villain? The blue *kumadori* lines of the makeup indicate that the character is a ghost. If we refer back to the story of *Funa Benkei*, we discover that, from the point of view of the Minamoto clan, Tomomori is indeed a villain since he was the general leading the Taira forces in the war against the victorious Minamoto clan, led by Yoshitsune.

Costume

Once the makeup for Tomomori is complete, I go on to the costume. Younger actors help me put it on starting with some special cotton padding that makes the body look bigger. For an *aragoto*-style role, such as this one, many costuming effects contribute to giving the character a larger-than-life appearance. As the dressing proceeds, I give a commentary on kabuki costume.

Here, before going into the specifics of special costumes, I will give a brief history of Japanese clothing.

During the Nara (710–784) and Heian (784–897) periods, the types of clothing that could be worn were strictly controlled by the court. At that time there were three types of official clothing: ceremonial dress, court dress (used when in attendance at the Imperial court), and uniforms. The form and color of clothing for Imperial princes, nobility, court officials, commoners and slaves were all regulated. We know this from both archeological evidence and existing examples. The nobility received silk in the form of brocade, damask and silk gauze from the government.

Male commoners wore a kind of coat called a *koromo* and coarse *hakama* trousers. Examples of these have been preserved since the Heian period in the Imperial treasure house, the Shosoin, in Nara. Low-ranking government functionaries and laborers were assigned clothing called *joi* made from specially stamped cloth. Preserved examples show that this clothing became rather shabby, as they have been heavily mended at the sleeves and hems. When they were finally worn out, they were returned to the government.

By looking at wall paintings in the grave mound at Takamatsu, which is thought to date to around the eighth century, we can see that women also wore a two-piece garment, consisting of a *koromo* coat and a kind of long skirt called a *mo*. The women shown in these wall paintings do not appear to be of particularly high social status. Silk was reserved for the upper nobility. Most people of the time wore linen. In particular, women wore a kind of linen cloth called *kantoi*, or an even coarser cloth made from bark fibers.

From the Nara period, which began in A.D. 710, through

the Heian period, which began in A.D. 784, people of high social status wore exactly the same clothing as that worn in Tang dynasty China. Beginning in the Heian period, written and painted records show the gradual development of a new style of dress. The urbane and cultured Emperor Uda (reigned 888–897) moved Japan from its cultural adolescence when he changed the cycle of annual court rituals—previously based on continental models—making them fit Japanese climate and customs.

During the Tumulus (*Kofun*) period (A.D. 400–710), people had worn something like a Western-style gown as clothing for the upper body which, unlike modern kimono, closed with the right side over the left. Emperor Uda adapted the form and established it as court dress in banquets that he called *Miyabi no En* (Feasts of Elegance). Emperor Uda is also credited with establishing the custom of holding the Peach Festival on the third day of the third month, and boy's day on the fifth day of the fifth month. In other words, he took native Japanese festivals and transformed them into court ceremonies, creating a new courtly style that was Japanese, not Chinese.

This might be a useful place to make some comments on the difference between noh and kabuki costumes. Noh costume is never referred to as *isho*, or "costume." Instead, the word used is *shozoku*, meaning "clothing," particularly the elegant robes of the nobility. This distinction sums up the difference between the worlds of noh and kabuki drama. Noh is a refined art form perfected at the beginning of the fourteenth century by the samurai class; kabuki was formed in the seventeenth century as an art form for the common people.

The common Japanese kimono is formed by sewing together, side by side, pieces of cloth comprising the entire width of a bolt. The standard loom of earlier times was quite narrow, about 1 *shaku* (33 cm), but some members of the wealthy class owned looms that could produce cloth as wide as 2 *shaku* 4 *sun* (78 cm). These wider looms were needed to produce cloth for the much fuller costumes worn by the nobility, some examples of which are preserved in the Shosoin store house in Nara. The cloth is also stiffly brocaded, and the difference in width and stiffness can be clearly seen by comparing noh and kabuki costumes. The ordinary kimono, the kimono worn in kabuki, is wrapped around the body, first placing the right flap on the left hip and then bringing the left flap across so that it's edge runs down the right side of the body. It is customary to raise the right edge slightly, so that the hem of the kimono is not quite parallel to the floor. Even slanted in this way, the edge of the kimono will go beyond the edge of the wearer's body. The heavy cloth of the noh kimono, however, is so wide that the overlapping edge may project as much as twenty centimeters.

As I mentioned above, modern Japanese are taught that a kimono is to be worn with the left side over the right. Only when a person dies is a kimono put on with the right side over the left—a custom established by edict in the Heian period.

Many stage terms suggest the idea of the predominance of the left. The left side of the stage from the actor's point of view is called the *kami za*, or "upper seat." The right side is called the *shimo za* or "lower seat." When the Imperial court is shown on stage, the more important Minister of the Left sits at the *kami za*, while the Minister of the Right sits at the *shimo za*. The Emperor sits in the center. When walking forward, one starts with the left foot, when retreating one begins with the right foot.

On the festival of the third day of the third month (the Doll or Peach Festival), homes in Japan display a step-like stand on which is arranged a set of dolls that represents the Imperial court. For more than a thousand years, the highest-ranking dolls sat on the top step, the male doll on the left and the female doll on the right. During the Meiji period (1868–1912), as American and European ways of thinking entered Japan, the Meiji Emperor changed this custom by having his empress sit at his left. A certain department store followed suit by changing its traditional doll displays to match the emperor's initiative. When it set up its doll display in its show window it put the female doll on the left and the male doll on the right. Although this has become the usual arrangement, it is not the traditional seating pattern in which the left side is considered more honorable.

Perhaps this shift is a good example of the kind of cycle that customs can follow. The early Japanese nobility patterned their customs after Tang China. Then, during the Heian period, enough cultural confidence was developed to incorporate older

native practices into a new set of customs which have continued
to underscore Japanese daily life. Later strong cultural influence
from the West had its own effects, like the case of the arrangement of the dolls mentioned above. New customs will undoubtedly continue to enter, affect, and eventually be in-
tegrated into, Japanese culture.

To many people the kimono is a symbol of Japanese culture.
There are two basic types of kimono; the *yukata*, worn in the
heat of summer; and the *awase*, worn during the cold winters.
Both are perfectly suited in shape and fabric to Japan's climate.

Linen was the fabric used for the summer *yukata* from the
eighth century through to the fourteenth century. It was an important material that could be requisitioned and sent to government offices as a form of tax payment. Linen fibers are,
however, rough against the skin and eventually cotton took its
place for fabrics to be worn next to the skin. The cotton *yukata*
is the perfect garment to wear during Japan's summer, with its
high (more than thirty degrees on many days) temperatures and
humidity (often more than eighty percent). Anyone wearing a
suit and tie on such days will end up drenched in sweat.

Conversely, in winter the temperature can drop to zero
degrees centigrade. The everyday kimono outfit for such days is
the silk *awase* topped with a *haori* coat. On even colder days, we
might add a woollen overcoat for extra warmth. Woollen cloth is
a quite recent innovation—it was among the items introduced
through trade with the West, first with Portugal in the form of a
cloth known as *rasha*. Its use became widespread only during the
Meiji period. On the other hand, silk has been imported from
China for centuries, and today's formal *awase* is made of the
same kind of cloth that was used for formal wear in the Chinese
style in the Nara period. The design, of course, is now totally
Japanese, with the wide sleeves and open cut that allows air to
flow through naturally.

Unlike the cotton *yukata*, which is now rarely seen on the
streets during summer, the silk *awase* can still be seen fairly frequently during winter (some people still wear wool *awase*, but
these are no longer considered stylish, and a kabuki actor would
hardly ever wear one). Kabuki actors frequently go about in formal kimono, the silk *awase* embroidered with their crests that

are worn on such ceremonial occasions as visits to important persons on New Year's Day, and at weddings or funerals.

When an actor enters the *gakuya* dressing room, he immediately changes into kimono—*yukata* in the summer, and *awase* in the winter. He wears kimono whenever he is out of costume, and this is how he begins to put himself into the Edo period. We say that there is *ke* and *hare* to kimono: *ke* means everyday dress, such as the ordinary *awase*; and *hare* refers to the clothing for formal occasions, or the silk *awase*.

The *awase* worn in an *aragoto* role has between the face and the lining a thick layer of cotton wadding. Even in the middle of summer an actor wears this thickly padded costume, which can make even a skinny actor look as enormous as a sumo wrestler. Dressed this way, an actor's movements naturally become slow and exaggerated, a characteristic that Danjuro exploited to the utmost in creating the *aragoto* style.

There are elements of Shinto ritual in this *aragoto* style, and it is thought that Danjuro, who was known to have been a fervent believer in Shinto deities, may have intended the parallel quite specifically. Certainly, his strong affinity for the Fudo deity enshrined at Narita was so well-known that it provided the basis for the *yago* "Narita-ya," used to applaud actors of Danjuro's line.

Links between the Japanese performing arts and religion have a long history; at the beginning of the eighth century, the word now used to refer to kabuki actors, *yakusha*, meant "one who serves the gods." The founder of the sect of *yamabushi* mountain priests, En no Gyoja, includes the same ideographs amongst his titles; and during the Kamakura period certain priests who traced their line back to En no Gyoja played the *biwa* lute and recited tales of the battles between the Taira and Minamoto clans. These priests eventually ceased to perform any religious functions at all, and became actors and performers—by the seventeenth century they had come to be contemptuously referred to as "performing beggars." The noh drama developed by the samurai class in the fourteenth century, however, has its philosophical background in Buddhism.

The strong motivation behind the creation of the *aragoto* style comes through in many ways other than the impressive physical presence created by the costume and makeup. I have found training in *aragoto* an excellent vehicle through which to introduce to workshop students both the fundamental points of movement, and also something of the inner essence of kabuki acting.

Kuruma Biki is a representative *aragoto* scene which is used in the training program at the National Theater, and also for workshops overseas.

FOOTWEAR AND WALKING

To return to a more basic aspect of kabuki costume, we might look at footwear, the white *tabi* worn by actors. These are something like socks, divided between the big toe and the rest of the toes so that they can be worn with *zori* sandals. Sometimes a role is played barefoot, for example that of a geisha or a courtesan. Even modern geisha, while they might wear *tabi* in winter when traveling outdoors, will take them off the instant they arrive at the parlor where they are to entertain. I observed this myself when, in the 1950s, I was taking *shamisen* lessons in an area of Tokyo called Kagurazaka where geisha still gather. During New Year's greeting parties at the *machiai*, the restaurants where customers meet with geisha, I noticed that the groups of geisha who came to offer New Year's greetings all took off their *tabi* out in the hallway. When asked why they did this, they could only say that it was a custom they had been taught.

In the Edo period, good *tabi* were quite precious, and commoners must have used them only with great care. Earlier *tabi*, in the Kamakura period of the twelfth century, were made from animal skins, but cloth *tabi* became the custom during the Edo period—white for indoors and black for outdoors. As so many woodblock prints from this period illustrate, commoners usually wore sandals without *tabi*.

Since 1660, kabuki has been acted entirely by men. Actors playing female roles must walk with tiny steps, not only because a masculine stride would destroy the effectiveness of their acting, but also because a woman's kimono is wrapped quite tightly around her so that only little steps can be taken. After long experience in trying to walk beautifully in narrow kimonos, *on-*

nagata (female role specialists) perfected their own special version of the *suri ashi* sliding step. With their knees kept close together, and barely lifting their feet, they take little steps, walking with their feet turned gracefully inward.

This walking style is important for male roles, too, since samurai and commoners move differently. Samurai on duty always wore the *hakama* divided skirt, with the two swords that marked their status worn in the waistband. The shorter sword was always kept there, and the longer one was only ever removed when the samurai entered a house. To counterbalance the effect of the two swords at his waist, a samurai had to walk with his knees slightly bent. Although *hakama* do not restrict movement like the tight kimono does, samurai are never seen running on the kabuki stage.

When telling a trainee to take the position for a samurai walk—with the knees slightly bent, and the body's center of gravity lowered—we say *koshi o ireru*. This is the same posture that is needed to work in muddy rice fields—the muddy ground is so soft that farmers have to wear clogs, called *kanjiki* or *tageta*, in which it is impossible to run. To walk at all you have, as I learnt during two and a half years experience on the farm I was evacuated to during World War II, to bend the knees slightly, keep your weight low, and move with sliding, *suri ashi*-like steps.

Other people in the Edo period not only ran, but were engaged in trades that depended on running: the litter-carriers on the famous Tokaido highway route, and the messengers called *hikyaku* who delivered messages, money and parcels. Again a social distinction is demonstrated—those of the higher classes moved in a slow, dignified way using the *suri ashi* sliding step, while the lower classes ran about busily, with the hems of their kimono tucked up into waist sashes and their bare feet in *zori*.

DEMONSTRATION OF TOMOMORI'S DANCE IN *FUNA BENKEI*

The workshop audience is given appropriate portions of all this information while the costume for Tomomori is being put on. When ready, I take up the halberd and move to my position for the start of this part of the demonstration.

What I present is an abbreviated version of Tomomori's dance. This is done for two reasons: for audiences not yet accustomed to kabuki, it is better not to overwhelm them with anything too long, and in deference to the structure of the kabuki world, where an actor of my rank could never aspire to play a starring role like this on a major kabuki stage in pubic.

The dance for Tomomori is very exciting. At this point in the story Yoshitsune and his followers have set out to continue their escape by boat. The music conveys a storm breaking out and the chorus describes how, through the clouds, the people in the boat can see a frightening, mysterious figure approaching. It is the ghost of Tomomori, hoping to vent the hatred of the Taira clan by pulling Yoshitsune down into the very same waves where they perished. I enter waving the halberd and perform the swift dance showing Tomomori's attack and his defeat by the strength of the Buddhist prayers offered by Yoshitsune's companion Benkei.

After the dance is over, I take advantage of the fact that my son is a professional noh dancer and have him perform a short noh dance. This not only gives the audience the rare opportunity to see kabuki and noh side by side and compare the differences, but it also gives me time to remove my costume and makeup. When I return, now dressed in a formal crested *awase* and *hakama* divided skirt, I answer questions from the audience. Many of the answers to the questions are covered by the explanations in other parts of this book, so that as you read, you might imagine yourself amongst a crowd of people who have just been thrilled by their first close brush with kabuki.

Finally, since ceremony is always important in Japan, I perform a short auspicious dance and the kabuki workshop draws to a close.

A KABUKI SYLLABUS

The demonstration workshop is not the only way to teach kabuki. In addition to bringing kabuki closer to a general audience through this kind of workshop/performance, more systematic training sessions are offered both in Japan and overseas. The following are notes from a typical training program, a series of lessons in etiquette and deportment given at Showa Music Conservatory.

Etiquette and deportment are the very foundation of kabuki

movement, and for a foreign class which has never witnessed Japanese ways of sitting, walking and bowing, this is especially important. Strangely enough, these Japanese ways have become just as unfamiliar to many modern Japanese so that a training program for them has to begin in the same way.

The Sliding Walk

Always enter the dance studio or practice room from the left side of the room—the side corresponding to stage right. On stage, stage left is considered the more prestigious side and so by entering the room from the less important side one shows humility.

One should walk using the sliding step (*suri ashi*), in which the soles of the feet maintain constant contact with the floor. The toes should be raised as little as possible while walking.

Sitting

First lower the right knee to the floor, then the left knee, and kneel in the *kiza* position. In *kiza*, the toes are bent back so that the bottom of the toes touch the floor. Next, straighten out the toes of first the right and then the left foot, and kneel in the *seiza* position. In *seiza*, formal kneeling, the feet are folded under the body and the tops of the toes are in contact with the ground. Women should kneel with their knees touching each other. Men's knees should be far enough apart to insert two fists.

The Eyes and Hands

As one kneels, both hands should be placed on the uppermost part of the thighs, with thumbs tucked up just under the index finger.

When sitting formally one's gaze should be directed to different points according to the status relationship between the parties present:

1) If sitting facing a friend or an equal, look into his or her eyes.
2) If sitting facing a superior, keep eyes slightly lowered, directed at the spot exactly halfway between his or her shoulders.
3) To show special respect to the person opposite, keep eyes down to the level of the center of his or her chest.

Bowing

First of all, bowing is accomplished by bending and lowering the body, leading with the chest. It is important to keep the back straight and not let the head droop. Both hands are placed on the floor in front of the knees, forming an inverted "V" shape.

Breathing

1) Breathe in while bowing.
2) Breathe out while holding the low position of the bow.
3) Breathe in while straightening up.

Standing Up

1) Move the left foot so that the toes are on the floor and ready to stand.
2) Ready the big toe of the right foot for standing—this is a return to the *kiza* kneeling position.
3) Raise the left knee.
4) Raise the right knee and continue to straighten up.

Bowing

Kiza

Seiza

Standing

Posture While Standing and Walking

The expression describing how to achieve the stance of a samurai is *koshi o ireru*. The muscles of the buttocks should be tightened and both knees should be bent slightly. Lean forward slightly in proportion to the speed at which one is walking; the faster one walks the more one should lean forward.

The Position of Elbows and Hands

Women should keep both elbows in contact with the body, with the hands centered on the front of their upper thighs, fingers together. Men should separate their elbows from their bodies, leaving about enough space to insert a baseball between the armpit and the body. Men's hand positioning is the same as for women.

The syllabus continues with detailed instructions for different patterns for using the fan to indicate waves, falling petals, mountains and the like. After some of these basic instructions in movement have been given, students are taught a kabuki dance piece that not only gives an idea of its general stage movement, but also gives an idea of how different kinds of characters are expressed in movement.

After the basic dance, we move on to a classic dance like the famous *Fuji Musume* (The Wisteria Maiden). Although traditional methods of training do not go through basic exercises but start out directly with real pieces, I feel that it is important to give some basics first. But in the same way as traditional training, I soon go on to real pieces because this is the proper way to learn the fundamentals of kabuki, in the context of a dance or play. It is impossible to isolate a movement from the kind of character and kind of emotion that it is supposed to express.

Immediately after dance comes music, and so, after learning the movements of *Fuji Musume* the students learn to play the piece on the *shamisen*. In the Edo period people learned *shamisen* pieces by rote. This was especially appropriate since music was often a profession for the blind. In the modern period several special methods of notation for traditional music have been developed, and it is also possible, when necessary, to transcribe the music into Western musical notation.